CULTURE
and the
CHILD

WILEY SERIES

in

CULTURE AND PROFESSIONAL PRACTICE

Editor

Daphne Keats

The University of Newcastle, Australia

Culture and the Child:
A Guide for Professionals in Child Care and Development
Daphne Keats

Further titles in preparation

CULTURE
and the
CHILD

A Guide for Professionals
in
Child Care and Development

Daphne Keats
University of Newcastle, Australia

JOHN WILEY & SONS
Chichester · New York · Brisbane · Toronto · Singapore

Copyright © 1997 by John Wiley & Sons Ltd,
Baffins Lane, Chichester,
West Sussex PO19 1UD, England

National   01243 779777
International (+44) 1243 779777
e-mail (for orders and customer service enquiries):
cs-books@Wiley.co.uk
Visit our Home Page on http://www.wiley.co.uk
or http://www.wiley.com

Other Wiley Editorial Offices

John Wiley & Sons, Inc., 605 Third Avenue,
New York, NY 10158-0012, USA

Jacaranda Wiley Ltd, 33 Park Road, Milton,
Queensland 4064, Australia

John Wiley & Sons (Canada) Ltd, 22 Worcester Road,
Rexdale, Ontario M9W 1L1, Canada

John Wiley & Sons (Asia) Pte Ltd, 2 Clementi Loop #02-01,
Jin Xing Distripark, Singapore 129809

Library of Congress Cataloging-in-Publication Data

Keats, Daphne M.
    Culture and the child : a guide for professionals in child care & development/
Daphne Keats.
        p.   cm. — (Wiley series in culture and professional practice)
    Includes bibliographical references and index.
    ISBN 0-471-96625-8 (pbk.)
    1. Child development.   2. Culture.   3. Ethnicity.   4. Identity
(Psychology) in children.   I. Title.   II. Series.
HQ767.9.K43   1996
305.23'1—dc20   96-32160
                                                                  CIP

British Library Cataloguing in Publication Data

A catalogue record for this book is available from the British Library

ISBN 0-471-96625-8

Typeset in 11/13pt Palatino by Dorwyn Ltd, Rowlands Castle, Hants
Printed and bound in Great Britain by Biddles Ltd, Guildford and Kings Lynn
This book is printed on acid-free paper responsibly manufactured from sustainable forestation, for which at least two trees are planted for each one used for paper production.

CONTENTS

ABOUT THE AUTHOR

Daphne Keats is a cross-cultural psychologist with many years of experience in teaching and research with children in Australia and Asian countries.

Until her retirement she was Associate Professor in the Department of Psychology in the University of Newcastle, Australia. As an Honorary Associate of the Department she continues to supervise postgraduate students and carry on her work with colleagues in Malaysia, China and Thailand.

Daphne Keats has carried out many research studies with Asian colleagues and her own students in Malaysia, Thailand and China as well as with ethnic minorities in Australia. With Thai colleagues she co-edited the *Handbook of Asian Child Development and Child Rearing Practices*. She is a member of the planning committee for the Asian Workshops in Child and Adolescent Development and has been an invited speaker to these Workshops on several occasions. She also co-edited the volume, *Heterogeneity in Cross-Cultural Psychology*, the Proceedings of the Ninth International Congress of Psychology, which was held at Newcastle in 1988. Other books include *Back in Asia*, a study of returned former Colombo Plan students in Australia, and *Skilled Interviewing*, a guide for developing skills in professional practice and research.

While at the Newcastle Department of Psychology Daphne Keats was closely involved with the postgraduate programme in the Master of Psychology (Educational), training psychologists to work in educational settings. She is a Registered Psychologist in the State of New South Wales, a Fellow of the Australian Psychological Society and a former President of that Society.

In August 1996 she was awarded an Honorary Fellowship of the International Association of Cross-Cultural Psychology in recognition of her work in this field. She has been an active member of the International Association for Cross-Cultural Psychology since its inception, representing Australia and the Pacific Region for ten years and serving as Associate Editor for the *Journal of Cross-Cultural Psychology* for the past five years.

SERIES PREFACE

The Wiley Series in Culture and Professional Practice provides a guide for professionals whose daily work in a number of fields requires them to consider the role of cultural factors in the needs and behaviour of their clients.

Whether through immigration, urbanisation, the aftermath of wars and natural disasters, the movement of people around the world in the large multinational business organisations, or even the world-wide development of tourist travel, few are untouched by contact with people of cultures different from their own. Professional help is often called for, but too often professional training courses do not give much consideration to cultural issues. The volumes in this Series will offer some practical help for these situations.

The Series covers some of the most frequent professional situations in which culture is an important influence.

I. *Culture and the Child* deals with issues in child care and development. Topics include temperamental and behavioural differences, the family, social interactions, children's motivations and anxieties and dealing with children in multicultural social contexts.

II. *Culture and Communication* deals with problems of communicating in business and interactions in many different settings.

III. *Culture and Community Health* shows how different cultural orientations impact upon concepts of health and illness and so affect how professionals and patients can relate to each other for better understanding and health care.

IV. *Culture and Education* deals with schooling and the learning problems of children from cultural minorities within national schooling systems, but also sympathetically addresses the problems from the point of view of the difficult task of school administrators.

V. *Culture and the Law* takes up the different perceptions of culturally differing groups toward the legal system and the consequences in the legal processes.

Each volume in the Series has been written by an expert in the field who has had extensive experience in working with people of different cultures. Each has also carried out cross-cultural research in the field.

The books in the Series are designed for everyday use so have been deliberately kept to a modest size. They are intended to complement the accepted texts in the field and all assume the basic professional knowledge of practitioners in the field. Students in professional training programmes and participants in in-service development courses should also find these books helpful.

PREFACE

This is the first book of a series on culture and the professions designed to assist professional workers who have to deal with issues which have their basis in cultural factors. This volume has been written to respond to the needs of those people who work with children from cultural backgrounds which differ from that of the mainstream, especially those children whose culture is different from that of the professional.

Professionals in child care and child development can come from many disciplines: psychologists, pre-school teachers, youth workers, paediatricians, juvenile justice and welfare workers, family court counsellors, home carers, nurses and social security advisers are but some of the many fields in which the professional will meet with children from different cultural backgrounds. Inevitably problems will arise, and when the professional has children of many different cultural backgrounds in his or her care, as is the situation in so many countries today, it can be difficult to know whether the problems arise from individual factors in the child or have some cultural sources which should also be taken into account. It is hoped that this little book will help them to solve some of these problems. It does not attempt to offer ready-made solutions to all such problems, rather it aims to alert the professional to the kinds of issues which are likely to arise and offer some suggestions which may point the way to the professional solving the problem from within his or her own field of expert training.

It has been my aim to keep academic jargon and extensive referencing to a minimum. Because I write from the point of view of a cross-cultural psychologist I have drawn from the research literature in that field, but readers from other disciplines will no doubt be able to add to this background from their own fields. Yet it has been my own experience that few of the basic text books in child development give much attention to the culture of the child, and even fewer consider the situation of children in multicultural social environments. Hopefully this book will help to fill this gap, but it is not intended to be a complete text in child development. It is designed for students in professional training courses who will soon meet with the issues in real-life situations, and for workers who already are encountering them. It is a book to use rather than one to sit upon the university library shelves. It is this author's hope that it will also promote a positive appreciation of the great cultural enrichment that can come from working with children and their parents who are different from oneself.

To refer to all the sources which have contributed to the ideas presented in this book is well-nigh impossible. However, this Preface is a fitting opportunity for me to acknowledge the constant support of my husband, John, and the debt I owe to my many colleagues in cross-cultural research and in the study of the role of culture in child development. In particular I should like to express my thanks to Wan Rafaei Abdul Rahman from Universiti Kebangsaan Malaysia, and now of Universiti Malaysia Sabah, Fang Fu-Xi of the Chinese Academy of Sciences Institute of Psychology in Beijing, China, Chancha Suvannathat of the Behavioral Research Institute in Bangkok, and Singgih Dirgagunarsa from Indonesia and other colleagues in the Asian Workshops in Child and Adolescent Development for their support over many years of my involvement in cross-cultural studies in these Asian countries. In addition, so many ideas have come, both formally from their writing and informally in personal contacts, from colleagues in the International Association for Cross-Cultural Psychology. I can mention only a few: Ruth Munroe and Deborah Best in the United States, Cigdem

Kagitcibasi in Turkey, Josephine Naidoo in Canada, Bame
Nsamenang in Cameroon, Janek Pandey in India, Dennis
McInerney in Australia and in Britain Peter Weinreich and
Elwyn Thomas, himself the author of a future volume in this
Series. The reader will find references to these writers in the
book, but the more subtle influences which have imbued my
thinking on so many of the issues discussed are not so easily
expressed. I hope that I have learned something from their
work, but the faults and omissions are mine.

Daphne Keats
October 1996

1

THE ROLE OF CULTURE IN CHILD DEVELOPMENT

The aim of this book is to assist those professionals who deal with children whose cultural backgrounds differ from those of the mainstream of the society in which they live. The book is intended to be a handy, practical guide for everyday use. Although it draws mainly on the discipline of psychology, it is hoped that it will be found helpful for professionals in a number of related fields such as early childhood educators, paediatricians, social workers and workers with adolescents, especially those who deal with children from minority ethnic communities within multicultural societies.

In this opening chapter readers are introduced to some of the important ways in which culture plays a role in child development. Culture influences the goals parents have for their children and the methods they use to achieve those goals, and cultural values are transmitted through child rearing practices from one generation to the next. However, in multicultural societies family values and expectations may conflict with other social influences upon the child, and we open up some of the problems which children in these situations may experience. To conclude the chapter we refer to the cross-cultural research background which will underpin the following chapters. In those chapters we will take up more specific issues relating to the role of culture in shaping behavioural

differences in children, family relationships and children's social interactions, and their sense of cultural identity, motivations and anxieties. The first part of the chapter will offer
some analysis of the issue and the background of research on
the topic, and the second part will suggest some guidelines
for dealing with the problems that professionals have to face
when having to deal with that issue.

The theme of the book is the role that the child's cultural background plays in its development. What makes up a child's
cultural background? Certainly it is in part genetically determined: we are all born into a genetically determined family, the
product of both our parents, which creates our ethnicity and
biological inheritance. But culture involves more than ethnicity
and biological make-up, as we shall show more fully in later
chapters. One's culture includes all that makes up one's lifestyle – values, occupations, interpersonal relationships, the literature, the media, what one can buy, what one can attain,
one's natural environment, and the ways in which the accumu-
lated knowledge of the society is passed on to the next generation and modified by science, technology and the arts.

Today children of differing cultural backgrounds meet in many
social situations. Immigration accounts for many such interactions. In multicultural societies schooling brings the children of
immigrant parents into contact with teachers and children of
other cultural and ethnic backgrounds. Travel and tourism take
people to other cultures by the million each year. International
media such as television and film bring vicarious experiences
of other cultures into the homes and wield a powerful and
intrusive influence. Even our daily household needs are influenced by other cultures: food, household appliances, dress and
other items of personal adornment show the influence of other
cultures in the shops of most large cities in most parts of the
world. Because of television and computers and the global
trading companies, cultural isolation exists no longer. This phenomenon of the late twentieth century has enormous implications for all children growing up into the next century.

Multicultural environments will become the norm for children in many countries.

How can we understand better the needs of children whose cultural backgrounds differ from the mainstream or from our own? How can their interactions with other children and with the adults who work with them be made more effective? In many societies which contain people from a variety of cultural backgrounds such children can experience prejudice and marginalisation. Some become the butt of jokes and aggression from other children, others are victimised by adults, including teachers. In shops, public transport, entertainment centres and playgrounds they can be made to feel second class. Often external signs such as eye, hair and skin colour, stature and other physical features combine with distinctive dress styles to distinguish such children from their contemporaries and many judgements are made as to their behaviour, intelligence and attitudes on the basis of these cues. On the other hand, in societies which welcome cultural diversity these external signs can be regarded as indices of the society's cultural wealth rather than as threats to the purity of its cultural heritage.

The tipping of the balance between a sense of cultural enrichment and a sense of threat is often a function of sheer numbers, but may also depend on the relationship between the numbers and their distribution. However, there are many other factors which will affect how a society will accept the culturally different. As well as the external signs referred to above, language usage, food preferences and habits, motivations for school, attitudes to work, interpersonal relations, and religion are all influential. The values of society at large affect the children's perceptions of themselves and their cultural heritage, encouraging acceptance or antipathy towards the values of their own and other cultural groups within the society. Parents train children in what they regard as appropriate behaviour, but that behaviour is not always seen as appropriate when the child moves into other environments outside the family such as the school or the peer group.

Not only do children learn to absorb the family's norms and values, sooner or later they may also come to realise that their parents' way of life and expectations for their behaviour are not always approved of by others whose opinions are important to them. Younger children may have a vague feeling of being rejected by others but not know why they are rejected. If they are the butt of aggressive acts they may have no idea why that aggression is directed towards them. They can react in several ways: they can counter with more aggression, they can retreat from the situation physically or emotionally, they can attempt to appease their aggressors with peace offerings, or they can attempt to bring the offenders into their own play or peer group. Children will respond in different ways reflecting both their family upbringing and values and how they have been treated by others.

Teachers of pre-school children, child care workers and psychologists who work with adolescents see these behaviours many times in the usual course of their work. In this book we will try to give some effective ways of dealing with these situations. The problem is how to be sensitive to cultural factors but prevent cultural difference becoming the sole focus. Within all cultural groups there is great individual variation and it is important to be able to treat each child on his or her own individual terms. When one becomes alerted to cultural differences there can be a temptation to regard a child's behaviour in stereotypical terms as expressing cultural rather than individual differences. In fact, these two sources of variation are in interaction: individual differences are both shaped and limited by the child's cultural background, just as in more homogeneous societies they are shaped and limited by social factors such as socio-economic status, education and access to social experiences of all kinds.

One of the basic aims of this book is to show how we can make use of cultural difference to enrich children's lives rather than treat it as a problem. By helping them and the workers who care for them to understand other cultures better, we can help to reduce intolerance and counter persecution before it develops into adult behaviours. Many will ask whether this can be done without dropping standards or sacrificing fundamental beliefs. To understand is not necessarily to condone, nor does one have to accept every belief or practice merely because it has a different cultural basis. It has to be constantly kept in mind that cultures are not static and even the most traditional are subject to change.

CULTURE AND ETHNICITY DISTINGUISHED

An important factor which needs to be taken into consideration is the difference between culture and ethnicity. There are many definitions of each and it is not surprising that the two concepts are often confused. The confusion arises when cultural factors such as language usage and lifestyle are included in the concept of ethnicity. Thomas (1986, p. 372) states,

> The criteria used for making judgements about ethnicity usually include one or more of these attributes:
> Ethnic self-identity – the label a person prefers;
> Ascribed ethnic identity – the label others give to a person;
> Cultural identity – the degree to which a person is familiar with and prefers a particular life style;
> Racial identity – based on physical appearance (e.g., skin colour);
> Nationality – based on country of birth or citizenship; and
> Descent – based on ethnicity of parents.

Thomas argues that in this list of attributes only ethnic self-identity is both a necessary and sufficient condition for establishing ethnic identity, that biological characteristics and cultural traits are not necessary in the definition of ethnicity. However, a distinction can be made between ethnicity and ethnic identity, ethnicity being what a person is and ethnic identity being what a person prefers. For the present purpose, therefore, a more limited concept of ethnicity will be adopted. It is proposed that an essential condition for ethnicity is a connection with a particular group through hereditary ties. A person who marries into another ethnic group remains ethnically different even though he or she adopts the lifestyle of that group and is accepted by its members. The children of that union will inherit the ethnicity of both parents, even if the ethnicity of one parent is not known to the child or is socially unacceptable to other members of the child's family. When this process continues over several generations the child may assume the ethnic identity of the parental home. In these situations some children do not have full knowledge of their own ethnic backgrounds. Many children brought up in the cultural environment of a dominant culture have grown to adolescence and even to adulthood unaware of their mixed ethnic heritage. It can come as a devastating shock to find that part of their heritage is from an ethnic group held in low esteem by those with whom they have come to identify. Ethnicity and subjective ethnic identity are not always the same.

Because cultural differences are based in behaviours, values and the material aspects of lifestyle rather than in biological background, a group with cultural similarity may include members of the same ethnic background but also members of different ethnic backgrounds. Within one ethnic group members may adopt a variety of cultural lifestyles. It is therefore quite possible to have within a group of children under one's care some children who are ethnically different but culturally similar to one another, some children who are ethnically similar but culturally different from one another, and other children who are both ethnically and culturally different from the mainstream.

In immigrant families it is a common situation that the acculturation process does not touch basic cultural values, which remain stable over generations, while external behaviours conform to the more general expectations of the society. For children this is seen very clearly in the conforming behaviour required in school situations, but also may be observed in their peer group relationships, especially in adolescents' food habits, dress, sport and leisure activities. To a large extent these are superficial. It is when these behaviours are regarded as symbolic of rejecting deeply held cultural values that the attempts to adopt the new ways become a source of conflict between parents and children.

CULTURAL DIFFERENCES IN THE GOALS OF DEVELOPMENT

The goals of development include both explicit, specific goals, and the more subtle expectations parents have for what they want their children to be. Some parental goals are for the near future, others are for what the children will become as adults. In every culture children are trained to grow towards these goals. The goals can take many forms. They can be specific behaviours, values and attitudes, relationships and statuses, desirable concepts of the self, the family and the community, emotional states, the acquisition of knowledge and skills, and material possessions, especially those which are symbolic of full membership of the society. We will discuss these further in later chapters.

In the Western world having a job, marriage, children, house and a car and television are some of the most sought-after goals, for their symbolic value as much as their individual significance. In contrast, traditional cultures such as Aboriginal Australians may regard the main goals as achieving full tribal status, acknowledging responsibilities to relatives and knowing the appropriate traditional legends and spiritual background of the tribe. Acquiring jobs and house ownership may not feature as goals in their own right. For many immigrant families, for example the Chinese in Australia and other countries of immigration, the goals are for the child to become better off than the parents, to have security, for the family to be able to take pride in the child's success. Thus the immigrant father and mother work hard at any job they can get in order to obtain a better education for their children than they had. The children are encouraged to work hard in order to join high-status professions and to excel over the children of the host culture.

In societies which are in a state of rapid change, many of the old goals held by parents clash with the demands of the modern culture which is emerging and into which the children are growing up. For example, the farmer whose family has been on the land for generations wants his son to return to the farm but the son wants to become a computer scientist in the metropolis; the parents expect the daughter to marry early a man approved by the parents and have many children, but the daughter wants to go to university, to travel abroad or set up her own flat away from home in pursuit of a goal of independence rather than dependence upon her parents.

The relative emphasis placed on these goals varies across cultures and from family to family. Many factors influence the parents' conceptions of what is important.

Parents' own status

Few parents want a lower status for their children than they have themselves. They may be resigned to seeing no possibility of their child moving to a higher status or they may want 'something better' for their children than they themselves have had. Where caste and rigid class systems are found, the status of the parents and hence of the child is determined at birth. Parents who accept the inevitability of their low status convey to the children that they must accept it too. These families are unlikely to become emigrants as they lack the resources to qualify for acceptance elsewhere, but they may well be members of an ethnic minority underclass within a multicultural society as, for example, in India.

Immigrant groups, on the other hand, frequently leave their homeland in the hope of making a better life for their children. They see as the pre-eminent goal for their children a higher socio-economic status than they have had in the home country. They therefore expend much effort and self-denial in pursuit of that goal. They envisage as goals for their children a better education, and a higher socio-economic status than they themselves have had. To this end they are often willing to endure lower status jobs in their new country than they might have had in their home country. This problem is compounded in many cases by the refusal of the new country to recognise their previous qualifications. Many of these parents counteract the loss of face that is entailed by thinking of the lower status job as a stepping stone to the return of the family to the status it should properly enjoy, which will come when the son, or sometimes the daughter, will help support the parents in the appropriate way. Professionals may find in these cases that the attitudes of the parents cannot be predicted by their present occupational status.

Effects of traumatic experiences leading to emigration

In the case of refugee families, the traumas of previous experiences of war, famine, political oppression, etc., colour the expectations of parents as goals for their children's development. Merely to have survived may be enough in the short term, but for many the former lifestyle of frugal existence and the anxieties remain long after the flight and the initial period of resettlement.

This type of reaction in the parents may lead to excessive anxiety for the child's safety, so that to keep the child protected from threat becomes a pervading goal of development. The parents' anxiety is then communicated to the child. It can be seen in young children, especially when they have only recently escaped from a stressful environment in the country of origin or have been refugees wandering from one place to another. Similar phenomena are seen in the stress shown by child victims of inter-ethnic wars within their own countries, as for example in the Philippines, Israel and Palestine.

Religious affiliations and the goals of development

Within some cultures little variation in religious affiliation can be observed. Some cultures define themselves in terms of their religion, for example to be a Malay means to be a Moslem, but in cultures where a wide range of religions can be followed it is important to be aware of how the various religious beliefs and practices may differentially affect the goals of development for children.

Where there is religious heterogeneity, the individual family may set goals which are religious, or secular, or a combination of both. However, where a more homogeneous religious affiliation is the rule, the goals of child development will be shaped as much by the religious leaders as by the parents. Moreover, as the parents were also brought up in the same tradition, the likelihood of serious conflicts of values is not great. Minor individual differences may occur in family practices and to a lesser extent in beliefs, but doubt or rejection of the religion would bring far-reaching conflict for both parent and child.

Of the many religions practised world wide, the traditions of Christianity, Islam, Judaism, Hinduism, Confucianism and Buddhism have exerted powerful influences upon shaping the goals of development. Within each we can find many variants. In modern societies there is also a growing rejection of religion for scientific humanism. Those who work with children of cultures other than their own need to be aware of the implications for the child of the family's religious background. Even many commonly accepted scientific concepts may be challenged. These powerful forces exert influence on every aspect of behaviour and cannot be ignored when considering the role of culture in child development. When associated with political goals and national self-esteem, as they frequently become, the mix is potentially volatile, and in some cases lethal.

Political environment and the goals of development

This is not a book about political systems, but there is no doubt that the political climate of the culture affects perceptions of what is desirable as a fully functioning adult in the society. Is the goal to be a politically active person, or just a politically inactive but law-abiding citizen? Are those goals compatible? Is the aim someone who accepts responsibility for participation in political processes, or someone who avoids political involvement for the sake of maintaining personal security?

When the children of immigrant families have come from an unstable country where war and factional uprisings are rife, and where even young children have participated in these struggles, parental goals of child development may not readily include active political involvement in the affairs of the new country. However, members of some immigrant groups attempt to raise political support for their former countrymen from the immigrant communities. This situation brings more difficulties for the children. Factional groups spring up, affecting children's relationships with other children. Examples abound, as with Macedonian, Serb and Croat or Northern Irish and Republican Irish. When these group differences become influential they lead to moves to set up separate pre-schools and school systems, even separate universities, as well as politically connected ethno-cultural organisations. These developments colour and circumscribe the goals of development for the children of these communities.

For children from indigenous ethnic minorities with a history of poor living conditions and limited political voice, the goals of development may well include the acquisition of political power as a primary goal.

Skill in interpersonal relationships as a goal of development

For many parents the most important goal and the sign of a fully socialised adult is the ability to relate effectively to others with whom they will interact in their daily lives. Some cultures emphasise this ability more than others. Moreover, this ability is expressed in different ways in different cultures and there are many variations found within one culture.

Where the maintenance of the group is regarded as more important than the personal wants of the individual, these skills are directed at producing an adult who can avoid disruption and live in harmony with others in the group. In patrifamilial cultures the hierarchical relationships between father and children, husband and wife, grandparent and grandchildren must be respected as paramount in the proper conduct of the mature adult. In more loosely stratified cultures in which these relationships are more individualistically determined, the adult is free to develop close or more distant relationships according to personal temperament and values. Social status within the culture also affects how much emphasis is placed on conforming to the expected norms.

Knowledge and competence as goals of development

Whether it is expressed in cognitive abilities, executive skills in business or technical abilities, many parents want their children to acquire a high level of competence in some field of endeavour. Hence they encourage their children to do well at school to pass the hurdles which determine their progress to the desired goal.

Yet for many children of different cultural backgrounds there are some serious problems associated with this apparently laudable goal. One is the high level of anxiety which the pressure to achieve creates in many children. Another is that parents can be unrealistic in setting the goals. The parents' goals may not be shared by the child, and many conflicts can result. Also, for some ethnic minority people traditional concepts of competence can be at variance with those of the majority in that society.

Gender differences in the goals of development

Where traditional social structures are strongly maintained, roles within the culture tend to be rigidly prescribed. Rites of passage are separate for boys and girls, and tasks are allocated in what is regarded by the culture as gender appropriate ways. For example, under Australian Aboriginal traditional tribal law boys undergo the initiation ceremonies which give full entry into manhood status in strict seclusion from females, tasks are divided into male-appropriate and female-appropriate, e.g. hunting for males and seed gathering for females, and many sacred sites are segregated, with some for males only and some for females only.

It is not only in traditional tribal cultures that such distinctions are found: in many cultures the goals of development promote gender-appropriate role performance and self-concept. Despite the recently emerging strength of the feminist movement in Western societies, the traditional forms of separate gender roles remain dominant in the majority of cultures.

Problems arise for the child care worker who is attempting to encourage greater role diversity when parents want a more traditional separation of gender roles. The issue becomes important when a traditionally accepted male role behaviour is discouraged, or when girls are encouraged to be more assertive or to aspire to higher level professional and economic roles rather than to early marriage and child bearing.

The age when these issues reach crisis level is undoubtedly adolescence, when the boys and girls have been developing their own ideas and have been subject to many influences apart from those of the home. In multicultural environments the peer groups, the school, the mass media and what they themselves observe in public places all serve to widen their horizons and can be a potential threat to parental expectations.

Some parents feel that appropriate gender roles should be developed as early as when the child goes to pre-school, and express concern if they think that the correct behaviour is not being encouraged. They see this occurring in a pre-school teacher's acceptance of boys playing house with dolls and girls playing with cars or engaging in boisterous outdoor games. Many pre-school teachers will recall visits by irate parents bringing these complaints. To what extent this is a culturally based concern or that of an individual family is not always apparent.

CULTURAL DIFFERENCES IN THE PROCESSES OF DEVELOPMENT

Even when the goals of development do not differ greatly, there are many ways for children to reach them. Culture plays a large part in determining the methods parents and others will use to bring up their children. The culture also provides the adult models which will influence the ways the children will be reinforced in the desirable behaviours and values. The range of culturally related differences in these processes is very great. When the parents' methods differ from the professionals' methods, the child can become confused, apathetic, or rebellious.

The most commonly used methods involve some type of encouragement, some type of punishment, and some degree of modelling of the desired behaviour. The methods used to encourage include giving rewards, moral arguments, expressing praise for achievements and promoting competition. In most cultures obedience to parents and authority figures is expected and there are many methods used to counter disobedient or undesirable behaviour. Most common are verbal castigation, withdrawal of privileges, physical punishment of varying degrees of severity, religious taboos and threats of withdrawal of love.

These methods can be found in all cultures but cultures differ greatly in what is predominant. For example, in the family where the parents have been brought up in a cultural tradition where physical punishment is the usual method of obtaining obedience, the children will be likely to be brought up in the same way. Also, in cultures where a strong gender distinction in what is approved as good behaviour is found, more 'masculine' physical punishments are often given to boys and more 'feminine' deprivation punishments are given to girls. Moreover, as physical violence begets physical violence in the boys, so the girls become more fearful and submissive. At the same time the boys' more active misbehaviour can be actually approved by the parents as showing spirit (e.g. *hubris*) and a mixed message is thus conveyed both verbally and behaviourally to boys and girls alike.

Age differences may also be invoked as a rationale for using different methods. For simple reinforcement situations where physical danger is involved, many parents who do not use physical methods with older children would use a smack with younger children. The typical situation is that of the child touching or trying to touch a hot stove or an electrical outlet, when the punishment must be immediate and associated instantly with and only with the dangerous action. With older children the approach of using verbal demands is more common in many cultures. These demands are frequently supported by appeals based on reasoning, threats or withdrawal of love.

Yet other cultures are minimal in their use of verbal directions. The child behaves as a silent observer of the adult model behaviour and childish versions of adult activities are encouraged in play.

These issues will be considered in more detail in later chapters which will deal with the effects of cultural differences in the teaching styles of parents and caregivers on children's social development and personality. Whatever methods are used, the child is not merely a passive receptacle but responsive to the motives and actions of parents and others and increasingly able to think for himself or herself. Of particular importance is the case of the mismatch between the methods used in the home and those used by the professionals with whom the child comes in contact in other contexts.

TRANSMISSION OF CULTURAL VALUES THROUGH CHILD-REARING PRACTICES

In all cultures, child-rearing practices have always been a major vehicle for the transmission of cultural values. However, in modern societies, indeed now in almost all societies, the role of parents is augmented by the powerful influences of schooling, religious teachings, and the mass media. In some countries the police and military arm of government exert an influence on values; in others political groups attempt to enforce traditional values. Yet another way for cultural values to be passed on is by the influence of tribal elders who are more powerful than parents. Child care professionals need to take account of the fact that not all children are the responsibility of their parents alone, but cultural traditions may be such that grandparents, religious and community leaders or tribal elders can be even more important than the child's mother or father in proclaiming the values to be adhered to by members of the group.

That the most revered cultural values are not always written down is true in literate as well as pre-literate cultures. Many traditions are passed on orally in story form or represented symbolically in art forms. For example, knowledge of navigation so important for seafaring people is not always found in maps and charts but passed on from generation to generation through legends and apprentice experiences which teach not only the skills but the values of respect for the ocean and its inhabitants. Hence the Pacific Islanders who travel hundreds of miles across the ocean without map or compass unerringly reach their destination.

The young child neither knows what the values of the culture are nor behaves according to a set of values. Rather, coming to know, accept and internalise the values of one's culture is a gradual developmental process. This process begins with the young child responding to simple prescriptions and proscriptions, then generalising to other similar situations, and finally recognising that these are abiding ways to think, feel and behave as a member of one's own culture. The realisation that others may have different values which may conflict with those of one's own culture does not come in early childhood. The tolerance for those differences is a later development, and one which does not always occur.

However, young children can accept different behaviour in other children if they are not told that the behaviour is wrong. It is often observed that children of many diverse cultures can interact happily together. In an atmosphere which encourages acceptance of others few problems arise. It is not so much because young children are tolerant of other values as because they have not yet a full understanding of the cultural values of others. They may react favourably to children of another culture who are always clean and well dressed or who want to share toys and play with them whether they speak the same language or not, and unfavourably to other children who are dirty, or who have runny noses, or who take things from them or push them around, but in doing so they respond to the behaviour not to the cultural values which may underlie those behaviours. They therefore do not generalise rejection of individual children by attributing their objections to cultural identity unless this is specifically taught to them by parents or significant others. This stage of the child's development can therefore be an important time for professionals for preventing the development of prejudicial values when dealing with children in multicultural settings.

At a later stage of development the transmission of cultural values through child-rearing practices becomes much more explicit. Generalisations to various classes of people may be expressed as sweeping statements, and individual differences then easily become merged into the group identity. When these are the attitudes of parents, teachers and other significant persons in the child's development, the end result of the earlier specific cases of rejection is a prejudice against the group and, by default, any individual member of the group. However, these attitudes and beliefs may conflict with the values inherent in other group influences, such as those of the peer group, the images received from television and the pop culture as well as the schools and the child's own reading and thinking.

It is at this stage that many young adolescents, confused and lacking in the certainty of their own values, rebel, run away, get into 'bad company', and argue with parents or anyone else who appears to thwart their immediate desires. To escape their dilemmas, playing loud pop music, video games, just 'hanging around' with other teenagers, and experimenting with alcohol offer some temporary refuge. The tolerance for these behaviours varies greatly across cultures and among families within the same culture. When these behaviours become unacceptable to the community at large the social

workers, the police, community services and other professional agencies take over.

How well these professionals understand the cultural values
of the societies from which these children come will affect the
child's treatment and the child's confidence in their good in-
tentions. All too often from the young person's point of view
these people are just more adults to boss them around and
foist their values on to them whether the young person accepts them or not. Nor does the gap become narrower when a
youth worker attempts to adopt the current language, dress,
etc., of the adolescent without also showing a real understanding of the young person's needs.

Despite the external influences of schooling, the media and
the peer group, the family remains the primary source of
values transmission. Family values affect both the goals of
development and the processes of development. Because they
influence the child from the beginning, parents transmit their
values in many ways. The expectations of the adult are passed
on as norms of behaviour for the child which the child later
internalises and finally generalises as his or her own values, to
begin the cycle again with their own children. For these reasons extended families and three-generation families which
live under the same roof are particularly well adapted for
transmitting cultural values to the next generation. If the
elders are traditionally held in high esteem, filial piety en-
sures cultural continuity. Rebellion is less likely, but when it
does occur it is far more disruptive than in the two-generation
nuclear family. However, in many countries in the process of
modernisation these extended family structures are giving
way to nuclear families.

THE CHILD IN MULTICULTURAL SOCIETIES

In this book we will be especially concerned with children
who are growing up in multicultural societies. These children

can be fortunate if the characteristics of the environment are exploited in positive and supportive ways, and it is hoped that some of the guidelines to be offered here will assist in providing that positive atmosphere.

So often the situation is seen as one of potential difficulty for the child, but it can also be one of equal difficulty for the professional. The interaction of two people, each of whom has limited experience of the other's culture, inevitably leads to a lack of cognitive clarity in many situations, to problems of communication and differences in what is regarded as appropriate behaviour.

Multicultural environments can be found in many places, both urban and rural. In many large cities such as London, Sydney and Toronto people of many different ethnic and cultural backgrounds reside and work in close proximity to one another. A plethora of languages can be heard, variations in styles of dress and food are great in number and quality, and people of different cultures mingle in shops and on public transport. Most children growing up into this situation will take these differences for granted, merely noticing that many others are different from themselves. Many children, however, have been warned by fearful parents of the dangers of mixing with or talking to strangers, especially if those strangers are members of ethnic groups of which they do not approve. The effects of this proscription can very easily rub off on the way these children relate to others who are culturally different, not only to other children, but also to the professionals who deal with them. Neither may fully realise the source of the hostility they feel to be directed towards them.

In communities where people are from many different cultures an appearance of tolerance is often the only practical course to maintain a peaceful life. Many inner city ethnic communities can exist side by side without much interaction, in integrated housing or in ethnic ghettos. However, tolerance does not always imply understanding or full acceptance but merely that one party simply ignores the other. This fragile state of co-existence is apt to change abruptly when one group feels threatened.

When there is a social status difference in which one ethnic group sees itself as being discriminated against by another, the potential for disruption of the tolerant equilibrium is great. The more powerful group denigrates the other and the children of each group are told not to have anything to do with children from the other group. Thus the barriers to multicultural harmony are put up and reinforced. Attempts to improve the status of the under-group are deplored by the more powerful as discriminatory and a waste of public money, etc., and typically their under-class status is attributed to the group's own fault. This is the situation for ethnic minority children in smaller towns where opportunities for schooling, employment and leisure activities are limited. A striking example is the case of children from poor Aboriginal communities living on the fringes of Australian outback towns.

Another situation ripe for the development of discrimination and prejudice against the children is where the local population is being outnumbered by incoming migrants from a radically different culture. Perhaps the most well-known example is the demographic change which has taken place in some English midlands cities where incoming Pakistani settlers have brought a lifestyle and a religion so different that they seem to exaggerate the contrasts and the actual proportion of newcomers to older residents appears to be much greater than it actually is.

Associated with multicultural environments is the use of different languages, in public places, in schools, shops, restaurants and hospitals. When the number of languages is great there are many problems for professionals who are engaged in the provision of community services. Skilled interpreters are not always available, especially when speakers of a particular language or dialect are rare in that community.

To what extent children in multicultural environments should be encouraged to use the language of the majority society or be encouraged to use their ethnic languages has been the subject of much debate. For many ethnic minorities the language is regarded as perhaps the most important evidence of their cultural identity and is used to preserve the culture in the midst of external pressures to conform to the demands of the majority culture. Language usage is also frequently used as a political tool. Political involvement by members of one language group may be resented by members of another, e.g. Serbs and Croats, and can affect relationships between the interpreter, the parent, the professional and the child.

In child care centres and pre-schools attended by children from many language groups there are not always assistants with knowledge of other languages. For example, if English is the country's official language, the pre-school teacher may have difficulty in understanding her children's needs. At this age many children are still learning their mother tongue as well as English and if the basics of one language are not already mastered their proficiency in the new language can also be affected. It is a fortunate situation where the teacher speaks the same language as the child and can understand the child's needs. On the other hand, ethnically based or language-based schools have been criticised as fostering segregation of the children from the wider community and thereby inhibiting their acceptance of and by others who are culturally different.

Professional workers must also deal with the parents, and many report having more difficulty with the parents than with their children. At the pre-school level parents' involvement is usually encouraged as a valuable asset but many mothers who must work often cannot participate in the pre-school activities. Parents of children who are in full-day care may come to the centre only to deliver the children in the morning and collect them at the end of their working day.

Another issue is the relationship with parents of the opposite sex to the professional. A woman professional may have difficulty dealing with fathers from some cultures. It may be difficult in such cultures for the professional to interview the mother without the father present, while it may also be difficult for the mother to approach the professional on her own initiative, and even more difficult if the professional in question is a male. Certain topics may be taboo in mixed sex company. Both religious and cultural traditions may be involved in these proscriptions.

Children growing up in multicultural environments are not a new phenomenon but they are a feature of a world in which the international movement of large numbers of people is ever increasing, be it by choice or necessity, for short- or long-term sojourn. In many countries today policies of assimilation of immigrant groups and indigenous minorities are giving way to integrationist policies in which pride in one's cultural heritage is being actively encouraged. How to make these policies work out in actual practice is not an easy challenge for the professional.

INSIGHTS FROM CROSS-CULTURAL STUDIES

This introductory chapter has raised many questions of concern but it has not offered many answers. Nor has the reader been presented with the evidence for them. In the following chapters we will examine these issues more fully, in the first part of the chapter presenting evidence from research and other work and in the second part offering some assistance to professionals in dealing with the same issues in their work.

Much of the evidence will be drawn from cross-cultural studies. In this type of research two or more contrasting cultural groups are used to examine the effect of culturally based values, attitudes or beliefs on some aspect of behaviour. Cross-cultural studies often reveal differences, but in many cases similarities in the underlying psychological processes are found. Differences are frequently a matter of emphasis.

Cross-cultural research also addresses questions concerning relationships among members of various cultural groups. These studies include work with recent immigrants and indigenous ethnic minorities. A number of these have been concerned with the children of immigrants and the adaptations made over two or more generations. An important application is the contribution these studies can make to improving child-rearing practices in developing countries which are in a state of rapid social change (see, for example, Suvannathat *et al.*, 1985).

In the case of cross-cultural studies of child development we find differences in both the goals of development and the processes used to achieve those goals. Nevertheless, when biological and psychological factors are considered together in the context of the time and the social milieu in which they occur, the differences in the children may not appear to be so great. It is perhaps for this reason that professionals can work so successfully and rewardingly with children from a wide variety of cultural backgrounds and that the children themselves can accept people who are different from their own parents and from themselves. That difficulties do arise cannot be denied. It is hoped that the following chapters will help at least to reduce their impact.

SUGGESTIONS FOR FURTHER READING

Berry, J.W., Poortinga, Y.H., Segall, M.H. & Dasen, P.R. (1992). *Cross-cultural Psychology: Research and Applications*. Cambridge: Cambridge University Press. See particularly Chapter 2, Cultural transmission and development.

Bornstein, M.H. (1995). Form and function: implications for studies of culture and child development. *Culture and Psychology*, **1**, 123–137.

Ekstrand, L.H. (Ed.) (1986). *Ethnic Minorities and Immigrants in a Cross-Cultural Perspective*. Lisse: Swets & Zeitlinger.

Segall, M.H., Dasen, P.R., Berry, J.W. & Poortinga, Y.H. (1990). *Human Behavior in Global Perspective: An Introduction to Cross-Cultural Psychology*. New York: Pergamon. See particularly Chapter 6, The developmental niche, and Chapter 7, Theories of human development.

Valsiner, J. (Ed.) (1995). *Child Development within Culturally Structured Environments*. Vol. 3: *Comparative-Cultural and Constructivist Perspectives*. New Jersey: Ablex.

2

TEMPERAMENTAL AND BEHAVIOURAL DIFFERENCES

Differences in temperament and behaviour can be observed in infants of all cultures from the first few weeks of life. When the mother reports that her second child is not as placid, or sleeps longer, or is an easier child than her first, she is reporting a temperamental difference between the two children. In this chapter two questions are addressed. First: Do these temperamental differences show themselves differently in the behaviour of children from different cultures? And, second: If so, how are such behavioural differences interpreted as 'good' or 'bad' behaviour by the child? We then go on to consider what the child care professional needs to know in order to deal most effectively with those differences. Some examples are given from a variety of cultural backgrounds.

TEMPERAMENTAL DIFFERENCES

Research evidence from many countries now accepts that culturally related differences in temperament do occur. However, their manifestation in behaviour is complicated by a number of factors. The wide range of individual differences in children within any one culture means that there will be a wide range of individual variation in temperament. However, cultures may vary in the width of that range, some being

more limited than others. Also, the ways in which temperamental differences are translated into behaviour will depend
upon many cultural factors.

Sources of temperamental variation can be genetic, physical,
environmental, and the effects of treatment. These sources are
not independent of each other, but occur in dynamic interaction. Both individual and cultural differences appear in the
distinctive ways in which those factors come together, not in a
static relationship but in a co-constructionist transaction in
which both child and caregivers mutually contribute to the
child's development.

Genetic sources are perhaps most apparent in the genetically
linked disabilities and diseases which have behavioural ex-
pressions which correspond to particular temperamental
styles. One example is the mood swings and unpredictable
loss of attentiveness in patients with Tourette's syndrome.
(This theme is beyond the scope of this book; for a fuller
treatment of genetic bases of this and other disorders see Lois
Wingerson's *Mapping our Genes*, 1990.)

Physical sources include health, diet, vulnerability to endemic
and epidemic diseases, living with physical handicaps as a
result of diseases and accidents or pre-natal neurological im-
pairment. Differences in motor coordination and general
physical tone are also sources of temperamental difference.
Extremes of height and weight for age in the culture are another source of temperamental difference, one which has its
most notable effects in the rapid growth spurts of puberty.
Although physical in manifestation, these differences may
have a genetic basis.

Environmental sources include the effects of home and
cultural contexts, socio-economic conditions, geographical
environments such as tropical, temperate or severe, preval-
ence of services such as water supply and schools, urban or
rural.

Treatment effects include the effects of differing parenting styles and expectations for the child by the parents, and treatment of the child by caregivers and others.

From extensive studies in a number of countries and follow-up studies over several years, Thomas, Chess & Birch (1970, cited in Skolnick, 1986) proposed nine dimensions of temperamental difference. These are now well accepted and have been found in much later research.

1. Activity level – High v. Low
2. Rhythmicity – Regular v. Irregular
3. Distractibility – Distractible v. Not distractible
4. Approach–withdrawal – Positive v. Negative
5. Adaptability – Adaptive v. Non-adaptive
6. Attention span and persistence – Long v. Short
7. Intensity of reaction – Intense v. Mild
8. Threshold of responsiveness – Low v. High
9. Quality of mood – Positive v. Negative

From these nine dimensions five categories of temperament were obtained: Easy; Intermediate–Low; Intermediate–High; Slow to Warm Up; Difficult. The instrument based on these dimensions and used in most subsequent research was the Revised Infant Temperament Scale developed by Carey and McDevitt (1978). This scale is a ninety-five-item questionnaire completed by the mother and/or child care professional. It has been used in many cultural contexts.

One of the largest programmes of studies which included infants from a multicultural context was carried out in Victoria, Australia, by Prior and her colleagues (Prior, Kyrios & Oberklaid, 1986; Prior et al., 1987a, 1987b; Prior, Sanson & Oberklaid, 1989; Axia, Prior & Carelli, 1992). These studies included infants from British, Western European, Greek, Lebanese, North American, Asian and Indian Sub-Continent backgrounds as well as infants whose parents were both Australian-born. Cultural differences indicated that difficult

temperament was much more common in the Greek,
Lebanese and North American groups, while the British,
European and Indian Sub-Continent groups reported either
similar or less difficulty than the Australians.

In one aspect of the research programme the findings from
previous American and Chinese studies using the nine dimensions of the scale were compared with findings for a large
group of Greek-background and Australian-background infants. American infants were highest on activity, adaptability,
and distractibility, highest on rhythmicity, and lowest on withdrawal. The Greek infants were low on rhythmicity, adaptability and high on withdrawal. The Chinese infants were rated
as more intense, lowest in threshold, low in distractibility and
high on withdrawal. The Australian infants resembled the
American in their relatively high levels of approaching, adaptability and activity. Research in Japan using other methods by
Bornstein and his colleagues (Bornstein *et al.*, 1990a, 1990b)
presents a picture of Japanese infants similar to the Chinese.

Altogether there would appear to be many culturally related
differences in temperament in infants, even when possible
differences in response styles and other issues of com-
parability are taken into account. To what extent these are
biologically based is not clear. It is clear, however, that the
infant's temperament may reflect the mother's. The Japanese
amae relationship is a good example. It is also true that different cultures may encourage or tolerate different combinations of temperamental styles. Obviously it is not possible
here to list all the variations that professionals will encounter;
the above examples may give some idea of the range and
complexity of the cultural differences involved.

BEHAVIOURAL DIFFERENCES

From temperamental differences in infancy to behavioural
outcomes in later childhood and adolescence is not a direct

path. In some children temperamental differences may become more apparent as the child grows, while in others the temperamental styles observed in early childhood may not remain the same as in earlier years. The child is being socialised into a cultural environment which approves of certain ways of reacting and discourages others. So, in a culture which encourages self-assertiveness and tolerates aggression, the active, restless child with an intense reaction style will be encouraged in self-assertive behaviour; aggressive acts will not receive severe punishment and may often be excused as high spirits. In a culture which prizes intergroup harmony aggressiveness will be avoided by discouraging self-assertive behaviour in the child.

Gender differences in behaviour are well accepted in many cultures. The notion that boys will be more active, more self-assertive and more aggressive than girls is widespread and is borne out by research in many countries. Both directly and indirectly, through initiation ceremonies and rites of passage, dress, toys and games, household tasks and role preparation, the culture passes on the messages that emphasise the desired gender-based behaviours. Temperamental differences in the child's nature affect the degree to which the growing child accepts, absorbs or finally internalises the gender role expectations of the culture.

WHAT IS GOOD OR BAD BEHAVIOUR IN A CHILD?

Cultural differences in what is regarded as good or bad behaviour in children can lead child care workers to evaluate children in terms of their own cultural norms rather than those of the child's culture. For example, the child who averts her eyes from an adult may be trying to be very polite, whereas the adult may interpret this behaviour as uncooperativeness or guilt because the child appears to be unable to look the other in the eye.

In cases such as in the above example what appear to be temperamental or behavioural differences may have a cultural rather than an individual basis. On the other hand, in multicultural environments such behavioural differences can set groups of children apart from others on cultural grounds, leading to stereotyping rather than treating children as individuals who differ in temperament from one another. For example, Aboriginal boys may be regarded as being good at sport, and, by implication, not good at school work, and most Asian girls are seen as being meek and polite, and, by implication, likely to be good at schoolwork. But what of the Aboriginal boy who is not good at sport but enjoys learning, and the Asian girl who is outspoken and a poor scholar? Stereotyping makes the recognition of individual differences more difficult.

How, then, can we recognise what is good or bad behaviour in a child of a culture that is different from our own? Is there some common basis that parents in all cultures want for their children, or do cultural expectations differ so greatly that it is necessary to treat each child as a cultural product? To what extent do these expectations differ for boys and girls? To illustrate the problem, let us imagine a pre-school or day care group of 20 to 30 or so boys and girls. In this group there are Indian children of Hindu background, Pakistani children of Muslim background, a Chinese, a Japanese, a Turkish child, an Indonesian child and a child from an African country, European children of Dutch, German and Italian background, American children from the United States, including some Mexican-Americans and African-Americans, and Australians of British background. Such a group may seem like a little United Nations, but this is not at all an impossible situation in an international school or an inner suburb of a large multicultural city like Sydney.

In such a mixed group of children a wide range of temperamental differences is represented: some of the children are nearly always quiet, others talk a lot; some persist at games and tasks, others can barely sit still for five minutes before they are up and running about the room or outdoors. Some appear to want to stay close to the caregiver, others stay by themselves in their own little world; some show tears quickly, while others are never seen to cry. Who are the 'good' children among these? One's professional training will have led to a preference if not a firm opinion, but will their parents agree? Should a child be encouraged to behave in what is not its culturally accepted behaviour? A further question for the caregiver and professional is to what extent conformity to some set of rules is desired.

To address these questions let us consider some of the most salient child-rearing practices and traditions of the cultural groups in the above example and their likely effects in what may be seen as 'good' or 'bad' behaviour of the child in this hypothetical multicultural setting. Because these outlines must necessarily be brief, the sources for each are shown for those readers who wish to follow up with further reading in greater depth.

Children from the Indian Sub-Continent

It is very easy for Westerners not familiar with the Indian Sub-Continent to make no distinction between Indian, Pakistani and Sri Lankan children. There are not only great differences among these three groups but within each there is a wide range of cultural variation. Religious differences among Hindu, Muslim, Tamil, Buddhist, Jain, Sikh, Parsi and Christian; language differences including Urdu, Pushtu, Hindi, Bengali, Gujerati, Tamil, Sinhalese, Punjabi and English; and caste differences among Hindus all add to the complexity of the cultural fabric.

For the Western professional in child development there is a great temptation to treat all children in the same way, 'equally' being thought to be fairer. However, while it is true that ethnic and cultural differences have not yet become divisive in young children, the parents will expect certain customs to be respected. Names will provide a better basis for identification than physical appearance although dress can be a useful indicator in some cases. Religious taboos must not be flouted, for example by forcing a Muslim child to use the left hand for eating. Fast days may induce some lethargy. It is important therefore to have some ways of understanding what parents from these cultures expect from their children as good behaviour and to recognise that their ideas may differ from Western norms.

The two largest of these many cultures are the Hindu culture of India and the Islamic culture of Pakistan. Each is represented in our hypothetical children's group, so we shall consider these children now in more detail. It is well to keep in mind also that people from these cultures are found in many other countries where they have formed substantial minorities for many years. Apart from a constant stream who migrated to Great Britain, many went to Fiji, South Africa, The West Indies, Kenya, Zimbabwe, Malaysia and Hong Kong during the earlier colonial period. In those countries they retained their ethnic and cultural identity.

The Hindu child

The picture that most readily comes to mind of the traditional Indian family is that of an extended family of which the grandfather is the head and in which the sons and their wives and children also reside in the family home. The wives have left their parental home to live within the husband's family. Seclusion, if not purdah, was the lot of the wife and gentle subservience to the needs of her husband and particularly her mother-in-law was expected. For every situation appropriate *pujas* were carried out.

In more recent times the situation has become somewhat different. Indian families have migrated to many countries and over several generations many changes have taken place in the ways in which Indian child-rearing practices have been maintained. Increasingly families are more likely to be of the nuclear type. Immigrant families may not be able to bring all family members to the new country, and in the second and third generation traditional practices such as arranged marriages become less frequent. Even caste distinctions can be forgone.

In the Hindu tradition children are highly valued as a gift from God. The most prominent child-rearing style is of a highly nurturant mother who is very responsive to her child. This quality can become highly indulgent, especially to sons, who hold a more treasured place than girls, who are in their parental home only until their marriage and are not expected to contribute to the parents financially.

There are wide social class differences. Lower-class mothers allow children more freedom to explore than upper-class mothers, but this is often because they have little time to oversee the child because of their own heavy burdens of work. This is especially the case in the poorer rural areas. In upper-class families the children are treated with great affection and often over-protection, especially the sons. In modern upper-class families there is also a growing competitiveness as traditionally ascribed roles give way to more achieved roles.

The consequences in the child's behaviour can be a high need for affectionate relationships, but this need may be obscured, especially in over-protected and over-indulged sons, by many self-centred demands. Children whose mothers have been highly responsive may look for more attention than the professional worker from another culture is willing to give.

The 'good' Hindu Indian child will be one who accepts loving authority, responds to the social situation by giving an affectionate response to caregivers, who will show respect to elders, have good manners and be obedient. The 'good' girl will be submissive and highly dutiful, and exhibit a deeply felt religious devotion. She will expect to become a good mother and may practise this role in play and by taking responsibility for younger siblings from an early age. If she expects that her marriage will be arranged, she will do so in confidence that her parents will make the right choice for her. She will expect love to grow out of marriage, not precede it.

For many Indian girls education presents both an opportunity and a dilemma. Role models of able, educated women abound, yet the properly brought up Indian girl must also plan on motherhood and, in traditional families, will expect to marry at an early age. For the less affluent and the rural girls, marriage is the only reality. Daughters in the next generation of emigrant Indian families may not be so acquiescent, and dating and boy–girl relationships are a cause of much conflict between these Indian adolescents and their parents.

Sources: Kakar (1979), Sinha (1995), Naidoo (1985, 1986), Verma (1995).

The Pakistani child

Although there is much in common in the child-rearing practices of Indian and Pakistani families, the religious differences between Muslims and Hindus mean that it is important not to confuse these two groups of children. Pakistan has as much in common with the Arab countries of the Middle East as with many of the cultural sub-groups of the Indian Sub-Continent.

Islam exerts a powerful influence on all aspects of daily life, providing not just religious beliefs but a whole way of living. The child's development is marked by a number of milestones, celebrated by rituals and festivals. In the more traditional, and the more fundamentalist, families there is a rigid separation of males and females, with women and girls in purdah and confined to the inner rooms and courtyard. In less traditional families there is much greater freedom of movement for females, the burkah only being worn outside the home. Yet others do not maintain such physical segregation or wear the burkah. These families tend to be from the more affluent urban professional classes. As in India, there are wide differences between rich and poor and between urban and rural children.

Boys are given more freedom and take a more active part in public religious rites and ceremonies, in accord with Muslim custom. If the boy is an eldest son, he must accept responsibility for his younger siblings.

What, then, can we expect as the behaviour of the 'good' boy or girl? Whether they have remained in their own country or have emigrated with their families, or are the second or third generation of immigrant parents will affect the perceptions of both parents and professionals. There may well be many conflicts between what the parents and what the child's teachers and other professionals regard as 'good' or 'bad' behaviour.

Traditionally the 'good' child is one who obeys his or her parents. A 'good' daughter will be submissive to her father and mother and will not expect to have free choice in marriage partner or in peer associates. On these issues the Pakistani girl from an immigrant family may try to show greater independence, causing friction with her parents. Modesty in dress will become a frequent source of argument. Some girls may be sent to segregated private schools but in mixed-sex public high schools interaction between boys and girls will be frowned upon. The wearing of traditional dress with the *hejab* (the traditional face-covering scarf worn in many Muslim countries) or complete covering will reinforce the girl's separateness from others, hence be a sign of a 'good' girl, a modest virgin, religiously devout and obedient to parental wishes. Within this constraint she may work hard at her studies but aspirations higher than those of the sons will not be encouraged.

Sources: Naidoo (1985, 1986); Naidoo & Davis (1988).

The Chinese child

What is considered 'good' behaviour in the Chinese child depends greatly on where the child has been brought up and for how many generations the family has been in that country. In Hong Kong and Singapore an urban lifestyle with much international contact and high-rise city apartment living is the norm; Taiwan can be urban or rural. In the great cities of China such as Beijing, Shanghai and Guangzhou there is also high-density high-rise living but the environment is very different from that of Hong Kong or Singapore. In the rural areas and more remote provinces a variety of traditional lifestyles and child-rearing practices can be found. Yet another group of Chinese children are the second and third generation of Chinese who migrated to almost every country of the world. In Malaysia over one-third of the population is Chinese and because of the former colonial policies the Chinese are urban dwellers.

With such diversity it may seem difficult at first to point to qualities in Chinese children which will help professionals in their dealings with these children. A first issue to consider is whether the family has become acculturated to a new country, and, if so, to what extent. Has the family become culturally similar although remaining ethnically different? The contrasting environmental influences of urban versus rural and Western versus Asian contexts also suggest different concerns and different solutions. Nevertheless, a core of values and behaviours remains in all these contexts which can be recognised as distinctively Chinese.

Traditionally Chinese family life was hierarchical and paternalistic, based upon Confucian principles of honour and respect coupled with reciprocal responsibilities according to one's status. In the modern Chinese family the 'good' child maintains the values of respect to parents and significant adults. Traditionally the father was remote and the mother close and comforting. In China today, fathers are more likely to participate in the child's upbringing but in some more traditional families living abroad the remoteness is still characteristic because business interests often keep fathers away at work for long hours.

Scholarship has been a way up the social ladder in China since the first examination system was introduced to select the mandarin class. Today Chinese children work hard at their studies, for their family's sake as much as for themselves. It is firmly held that all children can achieve if they try hard enough. So a 'good' child works hard and persists in the given tasks.

Material wealth was considered desirable to show proper status and thus it is acceptable to display or use it for the good of the family or group. This is an acceptable goal for the child to aspire to and in many countries the Chinese have achieved this goal. However, since the revolution in China the pursuit of material wealth as a goal has, until recently, been subjugated to the welfare of the group. For the many poor, merely to survive was the primary goal of adults and children alike.

A particularly salient Chinese value is the preservation of 'face'. In the group-oriented Chinese society any action which incurs a loss of face brings shame to the family as much as to the individual. Conflict resolution is frequently based on saving face of each other. Thereby the Confucian value of harmony is maintained.

Much has been written, and much speculated, about the possible effects of the one-child family in modern China. Fears are expressed that the one child will be spoilt with too much attention and, as more consumer goods have become available in recent times, that the one child will be given too many toys and other indulgences. This has been dubbed the 'Little Emperor' syndrome. However, research by Chinese workers has not shown much evidence to support these fears. There is no evidence of trauma; there is more attachment and more time is spent with the child. Mothers now spend more time with their child in its first months of life. Fathers also have more involvement in the family. The value of children has changed, and the child is no longer seen merely as another hand. However, in the remote rural areas where the policy has not been enforced the old ways still hold sway.

In the emigrant Chinese in many countries, the traditional expectations for children vie with those of the adopted country. Values of hard work remain and many Chinese children in urban environments help their parents in businesses such as restaurants and markets, staying up late and starting work early.

Another feature of life in the adopted country is the question of the maintenance of Chinese dialects and the use of the Chinese written language. Many second- and third-generation immigrant children have little knowledge of the language of their forebears. Where the Chinese language is still spoken in the home, children often become interpreters for their elders – a situation which can lose face for the adults.

Scholastically the Chinese children score well on examinations and ability tests and appear more often than other ethnic groups in the top grades of University entrance examinations. The habit of spending long hours in study is ingrained early, but the cost in anxiety can be high.

Sources: Child Development Centre of China (1993), Meng (1994), Ho (1986, 1994), Zhang, Kohnstamm & van der Kamp (1993).

The Japanese child

The young Japanese child enjoys a very close relationship with its mother. The concept of *amae* expresses a relationship in which an intimate dependence of the child upon the mother is created; but *amae* is more than a dependence created simply by caring for the child, rather it is a symbiotic interdependence of mother and child. Early childhood is a time of indulgence, going with the child's wishes and demands rather than attempting to control them in a dominant fashion. The expectation is that the social pressures will gradually lead the child to accept social responsibility and participation in an appropriate way. One effect of this relationship is that communication between mother and child is expressed non-verbally to a great extent, a style which develops into sophisticated nuances in adult social interactions.

Two kinds of goals have been identified, one group describing behaviours considered appropriate for effective social intercourse and the other identifying qualities helpful to the child's personal development. In the first category, a 'good child' will be mild, gentle, compliant, obedient, spirited and energetic, bright-eyed, brisk, prompt and clear, obediently smart. In the second group the 'good child' will persist, will endure hardship, reflect on one's own weaknesses, learn to understand and to understand logically. These qualities are cognitive but also stress achievement and are intimately connected with social competence. An intelligent adult is one who is able to relate harmoniously to others and qualities will be fostered in the child insofar as they contribute to achieving this most general goal. There is an expectation that all children will become socialised, hence the parent indulges the young child, melding the child's and the parent's needs and desires into mutuality.

The behavioural consequences are seen in the Japanese child's earnest persistence in approved tasks, and the mother's active involvement in those tasks. There is shame at failure and self-criticism is frequently used as a means of improving one's performance. Sessions of self-criticism are often carried out in the group rather than individually, the child gaining strength from the criticism. There is strong identification with the group, age-based and school-based groups retaining their influence for long periods and leading the child into the more sophisticated social group relations of the adult world. External forms and courtesies may hide deeper feelings. The cost for many children can be quite high levels of anxiety in both children and parents, communicated to the child from an early age.

When Japanese families move to other countries it is more likely to be as sojourners in the employ of large Japanese business companies than as immigrants. Japanese customs are maintained within the family even when the demands of the company require extensive interaction with members of the host country. It is in this type of situation that the Japanese child will attend a non-Japanese school or day care centre. Parental motivations may be as much to show that the family wishes to have harmonious relations with the host country as for the child to acquire the ways of the host culture. The foreign cultural environment may be extremely bewildering for these children.

Sources: Power, Kobayashi-Winata & Kelley (1992), Doi (1981), White & LeVine (1986), Bornstein (1995).

The Turkish child

There is a great contrast between the more modern and the traditional Turkish families in the expectations parents have for their children. Traditional families have more children and make greater distinctions between sons and daughters. The traditional Turkish family has been described as 'patriarchal, patrilineal and patrilocal' (Ateca, Sunar & Kagitcibasi, 1994). Sons are valued for the economic support they will be able to give to the parents, and to carry on the family name. Daughters are valued for the companionship they will give to their parents – especially for the care they will give when their parents reach old age. They aim to please their husbands, as wives the daughters also value having sons. Sons are expected to aim for the professions, daughters are not.

Characteristics most valued in children in both traditional and modern families are obedience and respect for their parents, trustworthiness and honesty. In both traditional and modern families scholastic success is valued in sons but there is a very great gender difference between traditional and modern families on this characteristic. In the modern families school success is valued for girls but not as much as it is for boys, whereas in the traditional families it is valued either very little or not at all for girls.

In the traditional families the most valued characteristics for girls are obedience and respect for parents, making a good marriage and becoming a good homemaker. Social relationships with the opposite sex are favoured for sons but strongly opposed for daughters, especially in traditional families.

From the above outline of parental expectations it can be seen that the 'good' Turkish boy will be expected to be obedient, but he will also look forward to a position of control within the family. To this end he will be encouraged to take responsibility early, to be a leader. He will be given more freedom than his sisters, especially in adolescence. He will learn his future role from the role model of his father, protective towards his mother and sisters but sure of his own superior status. The 'good' Turkish girl will have different characteristics depending on whether she comes from a traditional or modern family, but in each case she will be obedient and caring for her parents. Girls who have aspirations beyond the expected role of mother and homemaker or who want to have social relationships with boys will be likely to be considered problem daughters by most Turkish parents.

Sources: Kagitcibasi (1995), Ateca, Sunar & Kagitcibasi (1994).

The Indonesian child

Over a hundred islands and territories, large and small, make up the densely populated, culturally diverse and scattered nation that constitutes Indonesia. Indonesia is predominantly Moslem, but there are many evidences of assimilation of other cultural influences, as in the case of the Hindu-based Balinese culture, the pockets of Christian remnants from Dutch and Portuguese colonial times, and the presence of descendants of earlier Chinese immigrants and traders. Most similar is the Malay culture of neighbouring Malaysia and Singapore. Java is the most populous and is the centre of administrative and economic power. Most notable among emigrant Indonesians are the Indonesians in the Netherlands. Among these are many of mixed Indonesian and Dutch heritage. Another group within the Netherlands is the Ambonese.

Despite the cultural diversity, a distinctive style of child rearing can be observed, emanating from Java and influencing the direction of development in other regions. Temperamentally the Indonesian child is encouraged to be low in aggressiveness, high in nurturing of younger children and high in respect for adults and superiors. Javanese society is hierarchical; gradations in status are finely drawn and reflected in norms of appropriate behaviour within the family and society in general. The Javanese language also reflects hierarchical distinctions, with different forms to be used in accordance with the relationship between the speakers. Children are brought up to revere the two cultural values of greatest importance to the family, namely respect for others (*hormat*) and harmonious social relations (*rukun*).

Sources: Geertz (1982), Mulder (1992a, 1992b), Setiono (1994).

The African child

To the Westerner it may be difficult to appreciate the many cultural differences among children from Africa. Yet a vast range of cultures span the continent. From the Middle Eastern Islamic countries of the north to the multi-ethnic country of South Africa, from Kenya in the east to the countries of the western seaboard, we can find traditional, transitional and modern child-rearing practices. The influences of the former colonial powers remain in the languages spoken, and in the political, legal and educational systems, especially the influences of the English, French, Portuguese and Dutch. Nevertheless, traditional lifestyles are still found, persisting most strongly in rural areas, and expectations for children revolve in so many of these cultures around traditional roles and responsibilities within the family. These traditional expectations are often threatened as a result of migration to the cities, poverty, and, in many cases, civil wars, food shortages and endemic health problems. In those extreme circumstances perhaps the first expectation is for the child merely to survive. The situation regarding the provision of public education varies greatly from country to country. There is a great contrast between the sedentary urban lifestyle of cities such as Nairobi and the traditional nomadic herding lifestyle of the Masai. Yet within these conditions of instability much remains of traditional expectations.

In recent times many African families have emigrated to Western countries as permanent settlers or as sojourners. It will be important to find out the background of our African child before we can make any generalisation about his culture. However, some features of child-rearing practices are widespread. Social competence is a pre-eminent goal of development, and its criteria are based in traditional values which have a long historical basis. Children are inducted into their roles from an early age and a common method is that of apprenticeship rather than direct instruction. Peers, members of the extended family and siblings play a major part in this role teaching, providing role models for the younger child to observe and absorb. Stage of maturity rather than chronological age determines the child's advancement into a new stage of responsibilities. Children are wanted, and no matter how large the family grows mothers welcome another child. Because males are often away from their homes for extended periods, often going to a distant city to work, female-headed households are common, but because children are valued highly, children are always well cared for.

What, then, are the characteristics of a 'good' and a 'bad' African child? In one study Nsamenang & Lamb (1993) found that respect for parents, obedience, helpfulness, honesty, filial service and intelligence were cited by the Nso parents and grandparents of Cameroon as the signs of a 'good' child, while they considered that undesirable characteristics were disobedience and disrespect, laziness, fighting, greed, playfulness, fearfulness and inquisitiveness. However, many changes to traditional beliefs are now occurring, and it would be unwise to make stereotypical judgements about any one African child.

Sources: Liddell *et al.* (1991), Munroe and Munroe (1994), Nsamenang (1992), Nsamenang & Lamb (1993).

The children of European background

These non-Western cultures contrast greatly with those of European background, yet further contrasts within the European group mean that they cannot be treated as simply Western versus non-Western. The examples from our multicultural pre-school will illustrate some of the differences in temperament and behaviour which can be observed.

The Dutch child

In the traditional Dutch family stout independence combined with a strict morality have been the twin goals of child rearing. The Protestant work ethic fits the traditional Dutch value pattern well.

The 'good' Dutch child is therefore a hard worker, does not avoid work whether mental or physical, is encouraged to behave independently and has a strong sense of right and wrong. Dutch children are encouraged to speak forthrightly and express their own opinions. Education is available to all and girls participate at the same level as boys. Nevertheless girls are expected to become good homemakers and to learn housewifely arts through practise and by helping their mothers. Cleanliness is a cardinal virtue, especially in homemaking.

Dutch immigrant families have little difficulty in adapting to new countries which have British traditional cultures, as, for example, Australia, Canada and the United States.

Sources: Koops *et al.* (1990), Eldering (1991).

The German child

Like the Dutch child, the German child is encouraged in early independence. However, compared with Japanese, Indian and Indonesian children, aggression is more tolerated. Self-assertiveness is encouraged. At the same time there is much emphasis on correct behaviour in matters of manners and obedience to norms of politeness to adults and superiors. Technical skills are encouraged and high standards of performance are rewarded, especially in older children and adolescents. Praise is not given lightly.

Traditionally relations between fathers and children tended to be severe and remote, especially in middle- and upper-class families. Modern German adolescents are given much greater freedom. Adolescents share the pop culture of Britain and the United States and many learn English and speak it fluently.

Love of outdoor activities and physically demanding tests of courage and endurance are admired. Adventurous German youths can be found backpacking to many distant countries.

Sources: Kornadt *et al.* (1992), Keller, Schölmerich & Eibl-Eibesfeldt (1988).

The Italian child

Although also Western in cultural tradition, Italian child-rearing practices present a great contrast to the child-rearing practices of the northern European cultures.

Italian immigrants are found in many countries where they have established themselves over many generations. There has been much intermarriage, but their Italian cultural roots are preserved in the lifestyles of Italian emigrant families over several generations. Large families and the Catholic school system have kept up the Catholic Church's traditions.

There is no doubt that the Italian lifestyle is more relaxed than the German or Dutch. Emotion is expressed more readily, making the German and Dutch appear phlegmatic in temperament by comparison. In child rearing the closeness of family ties is stressed, reinforced in the home by obedience to the father and grandfather as head of the house and the central role of the mother as provider of food and cornerstone of emotional support. Despite the freer atmosphere boys and girls are kept under strict restraint. Strong family ties bring strong family obligations. In even the poorest families, family honour is upheld.

In this environment the 'good' boy or girl is one who helps the family, whether in the family shop, the family farm or in the home. The 'good' girl traditionally will intend to marry, as a virgin, and produce children. Today young women do not have such large families and although birth control is disapproved of by the Catholic Church it is practised nevertheless by an increasing number of women. With smaller families the traditional roles are changing. Eldest girls no longer have to take so much responsibility for younger siblings or do so much in the home. This allows a much greater emphasis than formerly to be placed on education which was not regarded as so important for girls. The 'good' boy will be one who will do well and bring honour to his family. He will be expected to assist, if not support, his parents in their old age. His future success in business, trades or the professions is directed as much to this end as to his own self-advancement.

Sources: Bertelli (1985), Cashmore & Goodnow (1986).

The American child

Of all cultural groups, undoubtedly more has been written about the American child than any other. Moreover, because

American children are the subject of so many texts in the field of child development and aids for parents, it might appear that what is said for the American child is of universal application. However, as the brief sketches above reveal, this is far from true. Within the United States there are many sub-cultures, not the least in importance and difference from the white European mainstream being the sub-cultures of the in-digenous American Indians, the African-Americans and those of Central America such as Puerto Ricans and Mexican-Americans, each of whom make up sizeable populations.

What the textbooks and the professionals say may not always accord with actual practice, nevertheless there are some basic expectations for children's temperament and behaviour which appear throughout this literature. One of the most well-accepted notions is that the goal of child development is progress towards autonomy, in thought, in behaviour and in interpersonal relationships.

Freedom of expression is encouraged and the child is allowed to express personal preferences from an early age. This is seen as an expression of a democratic relationship within the fam-ily. The American parent is also encouraged to emphasise individuality. A paradox is that conformity is decried yet American children are highly conforming to peer group pressures. The freedom of private enterprise to sell whatever people can be induced to buy is accompanied by great adver-tising skill and power, and influences children from an early age through exposure to TV, personal radios, computer games and, most recently, computer networks such as the Internet. The availability of these consumer items in the home contrasts with the limited resources of children in many other cultures described above.

The 'good' American child has been encouraged to be self-confident and independent. The American child is encour-aged to be active, to be confident in speaking out to adults as well as to other children. The 'good' child is resourceful in utilising the environment and is brought up to a mastery of modern technical skills such as using computers and electronic communications. In a middle-class nuclear family the child has many material advantages. However, the contrast between the well-off and the poor is marked and is very evident in the African-American and Central American sub-cultures.

In the African-American sub-culture larger families and strong family ties with a family network more like that of an extended family than a nuclear family characterise the home life of most children. Much has been written on the problems of poverty and colour discrimination, also on programmes of positive discrimination which aim to improve the status of black Americans. Despite such programmes the future prospects of many young black Americans remain limited. Physical skills in some fields of sport may be used as a route to social achievement when other routes are closed.

The other major sub-culture, the Central American or Hispanic, is typified in the Mexican-American child. Children of this cultural background are found in most large cities of the United States but form large sub-groups in the south-western States and southern California. Comparative studies of child-rearing practices show that there is a great contrast between Mexican-American and mainstream American families. Comparisons of values and child-rearing practices are frequently confounded because of conditions of relative poverty in the Mexican groups. However, when the variable of poverty is accounted for, many cultural differences do remain. Research shows a lifestyle which is highly family-oriented, stressing interdependence rather than independence.

The Native American Indian sub-culture is generally agreed to be a disadvantaged group, suffering from the loss of culture and uprooting from traditional environments. Children in many cases have little motivation for achievement and have uncertainty about their cultural identity. These issues are treated in later chapters. There is likely to be a mismatch between what tribal elders would regard as good behaviour and what the child thinks is expected by authority figures.

Sources: General texts on developmental psychology, e.g. Skolnick (1986), Pedersen *et al.* (1989).

The Australian child

The predominantly British cultural environment of Australian children derives from the emigration of English, Scottish, Welsh and Irish colonists of the past and the more recent influx of immigrants under current immigration policies. Despite the recent multicultural nature of immigrants to Australia, those of British background are still the majority.

The early arrivals found much that was different in the new environment. Climate and distance have contributed to temperamental differences. Although British social institutions remain the basis of the Australian society, American influences and the changes arising from the multicultural immigration policies now greatly affect the lives of modern Australian children.

Contrary to popular myth, the Australian population is not a rural one but one of the most urban in the world. Most children reside in the suburbs of the cities on the coastal fringe. All the major cities are multicultural; over 40% of children have parents who were born overseas.

What, then, is a 'good' or 'bad' Australian child like? Traditionally Australian parents want their children to become independent as adults. Rather than training the children to expect to care for their parents in old age, the parents try to maintain their own independence as long as possible. Yet closeness to the parents is also valued. Parents are the main source of values and norms of behaviour for adolescents and younger children.

Egalitarian attitudes are encouraged and girls receive equal educational opportunities, although some gender differences in occupation opportunities can still be found. Sporting and other outdoor skills are held in high regard, so the boy or girl with these abilities will be praised by adults and popular with peers.

Social class differences exist but are not as extreme as in many other countries. However, a recent development is the increase in the number of single-parent families. In most cases the parent responsible for the care of the child is the mother. Many such mothers also work and child care in day care centres, pre-schools and by carers in the home is common. Many young children have their first experience of children from other cultures in these centres.

Sources: Burns & Goodnow (1979), Storer (1985).

DEALING WITH TEMPERAMENTAL AND BEHAVIOURAL DIFFERENCES

The brief thumbnail sketches above are not intended to present a complete picture of children from those cultures, but hopefully they may illustrate some of the kinds of temperamental differences that the professional is likely to encounter. Our task is to deal effectively with the behavioural outcomes. To do this we must decide whether a child's apparently good behaviour is a sign of alert involvement in a task or represents an inhibited or anxious response. Similarly, one has to decide whether the apparent problem behaviour is an individual response or the expression of a culturally accepted value or response style. If we decide upon the latter explanation, the cultural meaning of the behaviour has to be determined. As these sketches show, there can be striking differences in what cultures regard as 'good' or 'bad' behaviour in a child: the 'good' child in one culture may be the 'bad' child in another.

Let us consider the steps in this process of decision and subsequent action by means of a hypothetical incident involving two children and two teachers at a pre-school. We shall avoid any preconceptions which might arise from the children's names by calling them Y and Z. Both Y and Z are from cultural backgrounds which are different from that of each of the teachers and from each other.

Child Z and child Y are sitting together while the pre-school teacher tells a story to her group. Another teacher is present in the same room. Suddenly child Z gets up and without a word walks out to the toilet. The other children become restive at the interruption but child Y remains quietly listening but with eyes averted from both teacher and child Z.

How is the pre-school teacher likely to interpret this behaviour, and then, in the light of that interpretation, how would she be most likely to deal with the situation?

The first teacher's interpretation is that Z's behaviour is acceptable. Z is handling an urgent need by himself; Z is showing independence and this should be encouraged.

In dealing with the situation this teacher therefore smiles approvingly at Z on his return and briefly explains the part of the story Z has missed. Y's behaviour is barely noticed. However, when asked, the teacher reports that Y was being quiet and obedient but was not showing much interest or concern at the incident.

The second teacher has an alternative interpretation of Z's behaviour. In her view Z's behaviour is not acceptable. Z is misbehaving, not showing respect to the teacher. Z has no manners; Z should not go off on his own but should stay within the group.

In dealing with the situation the teacher reprimands Z. She tells Z that he should ask permission to go to the toilet. It would create trouble if everyone wanted to go off like that. The other children would not like it. Asked about Y, the teacher approves of Y's behaviour. Y is being good, showing a good example of avoiding more disruption to the harmony of the group; Y is showing respect for the teacher.

To what extent are these interpretations showing cultural awareness, or lack of it? To what extent is the teacher's cultural bias influencing her expectations for the children and how do these expectations match with those of Y's and Z's parents? We will turn to these issues in the following chapter.

In this chapter readers have been introduced to the variety of cultural differences which can be found in children's temperament and behaviour. It is also a truism that within any single culture each child is different and one must be constantly wary of attributing behavioural differences to cultural factors alone. The little sketches used above to illustrate cultural differences in what parents expect as good behaviour are not meant to present a complete picture, but rather to point to features which involve cultural elements. It will be apparent that, although there is much diversity, there are also some common features, such as respect for parents, but these demands upon children vary greatly in degree. The reader is urged to go to the sources mentioned to obtain a more thorough understanding.

3

THE FAMILY AND THE CHILD

As the brief outlines in the previous chapter have shown, parental expectations for the child's behaviour are embedded in family roles and relationships which vary both within and between cultures. Today many changes are taking place in families in all countries. Many of the changes are occurring as a result of policies of modernisation. For example, in developing countries changes from agricultural and herding occupations to factory and industrial work have created new types of urban employment that undermine traditional family stability. There is a world-wide movement of migration from rural to urban living which divides traditional rural families and places stress on those who move from the rural to the urban lifestyle. In recent years many families have emigrated to another country, with consequent disruption of former lifestyles. Other influences affecting families include the mass media, especially film and television, the spread of national systems of education, and the many family planning and family support programmes that have been introduced in developing countries by governments and international aid agencies.

These changes are so profound in many cultures that some may now ask 'What is a family?' (e.g. Burns, 1991). Two major types of family structure which have influenced the treatment of the child within the family and the child's learning of its own role expectations are the nuclear family and the extended family. Many variants are to be found within each of these major types. In many countries the traditional extended family structures are giving way to a more nuclear type of family household and along with these changes in lifestyle come many changes in family values. A typical example is that of the changing family values in Greece (Georgas, 1989). In a personal account of her grandmother's, her mother's and her own role in a well-to-do Indian family, Verma (1995) points out how the changes towards a nuclear rather than the traditional extended family household have brought consequent effects upon the mother's role.

In many Western countries the nuclear family is the most common type, but it is now not as stable as formerly. See, for example, Funder (1991) on Australian families. Marriages may end in divorce, leaving a one-parent family; remarriage may occur with step-families developing; when the husband and wife each have children from a previous marriage, blended families are created. Another frequent case is that of the single parent who has not married. This may be by choice, but more usually because the mother is a single girl and the father is not known or has left her.

These variations in family structure are not usually found in cultures in which the extended family is or has been the cultural norm. Where there are strong cultural or religious prohibitions on divorce, family structures are usually characterised by ascribed roles and hierarchical, patriarchal role relationships. These roles are threatened when the cohesion of the family group breaks down.

In almost all situations where the professional must deal with the child, he or she must also deal with the child's family. Many would prefer to be able to deal only with the child, finding the parent from another culture difficult to understand. It may be difficult to engage in discussion about the child, but the professional may not know whether this communication failure is because of the parent's poor ability to use the language, whether it reflects a cultural difference in communication styles or whether there is some more deep-seated resentment or anxiety which is inhibiting the parent's responses. Many parents are shy about dealing with people of another culture and the professional may seem to embody official power about which their past experience has taught them to be very cautious. To the professional such reticence may suggest that the parent is showing unwillingness to participate in the child's school, pre-school or day-care activities. Not adhering to the professional's expectations of what is appropriate may be interpreted as having unacceptably rigid standards of behaviour, involving taboos and habits which the parent wants to enforce in the child while in the professional's care.

How, and why, do such attitudes arise? To answer this question it is necessary to consider some of the salient factors which distinguish cultures in family roles and relationships. These become crucial factors when a family moves to a different cultural environment, whether the move is from a rural to a multicultural urban environment or to another country as an immigrant or temporary sojourner.

Changes in traditional family structures and relationships have many interacting causes. When families move from a rural to an urban lifestyle, there may not be room in the small urban apartment for the parents or other members of the extended family, and older family members are left behind in the village. When families move to another country, either as immigrants or as temporary sojourners, to survive they must change some of their ways if only to fit into the daily life of the new environment. Again many of the older family members remain behind. Changes in the lifestyle of their own culture through modernisation, which brings new types of employment, also encourage the young to leave the traditional home for education and jobs elsewhere. As the rural people move to the cities, the towns and cities expand. The spread of urban development into what were formerly rural environments disrupts many families from their traditional way of life. Nor are the moves always successful: in many of the rapidly growing cities, such as Bangkok and Manila, thousands of families who have migrated from the village to the city to find work end up living in conditions of extreme deprivation. Political changes and ideological and religious pressures may also interact with all of these factors in varying degrees.

Some families in the transitional stages of the change from a rural to an urban lifestyle experience difficulties because they attempt to maintain the relationships they formerly had in the village. A common problem in this situation is that the senior members of the family or elders of the village are no longer available to solve problems or act as advisers on conflict resolution, or to give support in making decisions for the children's welfare. Women may be less segregated than in the traditional families but have less support from other women in the household.

A difficulty in interpreting whether such effects are the result of the move from rural to urban environments is that such moves do not come independently of other factors which may influence the break-up of the traditional family structure. One such factor is certainly the spread of education for girls, which can dramatically change their aspirations and their willingness to carry out the traditional family role expectations. This applies to both nuclear and extended families.

Changes in family structure involve changes in attitudes between spouses, between children and parents, and between siblings. What comes first in this chain is by no means clear, nor is the sequence always the same. Economic factors and migration, as well as the changes arising from the education of girls mentioned above, are also relevant.

In traditional families the expected roles are clear and separate. Responsibilities for internal household affairs usually belong to the females and external and financial affairs to the males. Children have responsibilities according to age, birth order and gender, or, in the case of West African children (Nsamenang, 1995), according to stage of maturation. In the large traditional family an elder sister may take much responsibility for caring for younger children and an elder brother will be responsible for the education and welfare of his younger siblings, especially younger brothers. In this hierarchy the oldest brother may be regarded as senior in status to the oldest sister even though she may be the elder of the two. Forms of address may reflect the position in the family. For example, in the Chinese, Malay and Indonesian cultures the names used are those which express this status rather than the given name as used in Western cultures. There are also terms for mother-in-law and father-in-law relationships which distinguish them from the person's own parents.

Within such traditional family systems there can be a wide range of activities which separate males from females in the family. Women brought up in traditional families may not feel a loss of power in this situation. There can be ample scope for the development of many household skills. There is also the recognition received for being a good wife, and there are many opportunities for interaction with other women which can be found to be satisfying. One of the effects of the change from extended to nuclear families is that this sense of having separate power fields can be lost. However, professional careers can be pursued by some women who effectively maintain the separateness of their roles at home and at work. This duality is available in many countries where domestic help is the rule. For example, in her study of the role expectations of Malaysian and Australian women students, Krolik (1981) found that aspirations for having wife, mother and career roles were not in conflict for the Malaysians, but this was not the case so generally for the Australians.

Extended family members often serve as home carers in lieu of paid domestic servants. For example, in Malaysia it is not uncommon for a rural girl to join the household of urban relatives as servant-cum-childminder for a professional family in the city. In return the urban family takes on *in loco parentis* responsibilities even though the girl's financial earnings may not be great. Sometimes this also provides the girl with an opportunity for further education not available in the home village.

Changes to the family after emigration

When families from extended family backgrounds emigrate to countries such as England, Australia, Canada and the United States where nuclear families are the expected norm, these family support systems are no longer available. In cases where family reunion is a feature of immigration policy, as in Australia, the older members may be brought out to join the younger ones who preceded them. This system has both benefits and problems. The older members are likely to have differing views on how the children should be brought up, especially in regard to matters of respect and obedience (Rosenthal, Demetriou & Efklides, 1989).

If the son has married a woman from another culture, there can be clashes between the wife and her in-laws. Matters such as what food is eaten, how it is prepared and served, manners, the clothing styles of the children, and allowing adolescent daughters freedom to go out with age mates and boy friends can all bring about family rows in which the authority of parents is challenged and the child is the target of criticism. The main source of misunderstanding in such situations is the mutual failure to accept the different cultural values of the other's roles and status.

It is also often the case that an older parent is brought out for family reunion because his or her spouse has died and no other responsible family members of that generation are left at home. While reunion with the son or daughter helps overcome the loneliness which comes with the loss of the spouse, in the far-off country another source of loneliness is brought about. Not having old friends and everyday acquaintances to talk to, and not knowing the language or the culture into which they are thrust, they compare their new situation unfavourably with the past. Their criticisms of the younger ones may well be expressing in an oblique way their own misery for a way of life that is lost and can never be recovered.

The children may resent the elder's interference, especially if they have grown to adolescence in the adopted country before the grandparent arrives. Myths about the former country which they may have built up in their imagination are suddenly dispelled by the reality. In some cases they have been told stories by their parents of the idyllic life of the town or village back home, the parents using their children to displace their own insecurities in the new environment but not admitting these anxieties to the child.

Another, but different, problem for some children is when the grandparents, now enjoying the luxury of having their grandchildren about them, smother the children with anxious over-attentiveness. Their indulgence may contrast with the firmer attitudes of the parent. Fears of the child being hurt or injured in rough play are expressed by discouraging the child in any risk activity. Another not uncommon tendency is trying to build up the child with extra food, constantly urging the child to eat and providing snacks despite the parent's wishes. This behaviour occurs among those who, from the deprivation of war, poverty or famine, themselves suffered hunger in the past.

A difficult dilemma for the child is how to deal with the problem of who is the ultimate source of authority when the messages from the two generations of adults in the family conflict. When the parent who previously was the child's source of authority with the final say is being over-ruled by the grandparent, the child's confidence in the parent is undermined. Confusion results for both child and parent. The anxious but obedient child's reaction may be one of meek compliance, obeying whoever happens to be the one who is present on a particular occasion, while other children will respond with sullen acceptance. Some will resort to lying and various forms of subterfuge, playing one adult off against the other with a different story for each. Yet others will be stubbornly uncooperative or take up outright rebellion. In older children and adolescents rebellion can then take the form of going all out to adopt the most unacceptable behaviours of peers in the adopted culture. Because of the patriarchal nature of some cultures such rebellious behaviour may be more tolerated in adolescent boys than in adolescent girls. (See Chapter 6 for a fuller discussion of children's anxieties.)

Sojourner families

A different case is that of the sojourners whose migration to other countries is temporary. This situation is found with employees of multinational organisations, foreign students and the so-called 'guest workers' of European and Middle Eastern countries. Not only must these families adapt to the host country during the period of their sojourn but they must also readjust to their own cultures on their return. Some families may have been away for several years, during which their children were born and grew to adolescence in the foreign culture. Where the parent's occupation involves many international postings, the children may exprience many different cultures within the years of growing up. Such families may feel at home in no country, even in their own.

In some cases only the husband goes abroad, leaving the family at home, while in other cases, for example that of the Filipina who goes to work as a maid in another country, the mother leaves her children at home usually in the care of other family members. Or a young man may find a wife in the host country and bring her back to the family home at the end of his contract.

The situation in which only the husband leaves the family to work abroad is typical of the majority of Moroccan 'guest workers' who annually make a pilgrimage across Spain from the Netherlands and Germany to North Africa. Where the traditional family structures are maintained, this separation is not traumatic because the children are supported within the extended family, although the husband may suffer from loneliness while abroad. The mother's feelings will depend on how she is treated by the other family members. Within the family group the children may find many substitutes for the absent father and have no loss of security.

In contrast, the Filipina mother's separation from her children is extremely traumatic. The decision to go abroad to work is usually the result of severe financial hardship and the large wages to be obtained abroad may appear to be the family's only hope of survival. The actual situation in a foreign country, especially in the Middle East, may be so different to what was anticipated that the woman suffers doubly – firstly, from the separation from her children and, secondly, from the difficulty of coping with a social system so different from the one she has left behind.

In the third type of situation in which the man has married while abroad, the new wife may be unwilling to go back to the husband's country but encourages him to settle down in the new country. With his marriage and a new young family the sojourn slowly turns into permanent residence. The children learn the cultural norms of the adopted country, or of the mother's culture if she is not a member of the adopted country. Such a situation occurs most frequently when there is a substantial minority living as a permanent or semi-permanent sub-culture in the host country. Some examples are the Finns in Sweden, Indonesians in the Netherlands and Pakistanis in Britain.

The cultural adjustments which these sojourning families have to make vary greatly. Studies show many problems, with language, religious performance and schooling differences being most prominent (see, for example, Eldering, 1991; Pels, 1991; Schmitz, 1992). In the host country there is often resentment against the newcomers by local workers and racial disturbances have occurred. Children of the guest workers may suffer ethnic discrimination in school and in neighbourhood play. However, in many European countries they may have better educational opportunities than in their home country and there is less gender discrimination. On the other hand, countries with strict Islamic state systems can be difficult for families of guest workers, especially for females who do not come from a similar cultural background.

When the sojourn is over and the families must return to their own countries, other problems of readjustment can arise, but these may be less difficult for the children than for their parents. Studies in Turkey by Öner & Tosün (1991) have shown that the major problem was in schooling where they were behind local children. Hatzichristou & Hopf (1995) found that schooling was also a problem for Greek children but the upkeep of the Greek language and Greek customs in the home maintained a strong sense of Greek cultural identity. However, negative stereotypes about the homeland developed while in the country of immigration were found to remain over time for many returning Greek adolescents (Georgas & Papastylianou, 1994).

Living with new neighbours

When families move to other countries by emigration or as sojourners, or from a rural to an urban environment in their own country, they frequently find that they must live in a more culturally heterogeneous neighbourhood than in their previous homes. The need for mutual support of members of the same culture produces ghettos in many large cities. Typical are the Chinatowns and ethnic enclaves of New York and Chicago. In some cases these locations are forced upon the new arrivals by the immigration policies of the country, as when new settlers are brought to meet some development programme.

However, many immigrant families soon find themselves in neighbourhoods where they are but one of many ethnic minority groups living in the midst of a host country majority. Typical of this situation are the multicultural suburbs of cities such as Sydney, Toronto, Birmingham and London. Here the immigrant families have to cope not only with the citizens of their new country but with members of the other ethnic minorities who can seem even stranger than the members of the host country. They may have had little preparation for these cultural contacts. In some cases, where war has divided a country – for example, with people from the former Yugoslavia – they may now have for neighbours people who were former friends but have now become enemies, and former enemies who have since become friends. The transmission of family values from adults to the children can be difficult to maintain in these situations of unsettlement and resettlement.

DEALING WITH THE CHILD'S FAMILY

In this chapter an emphasis has been placed on changes that are taking place in families in many cultural environments. With the shift from extended to nuclear family have come many changed roles for parents, and migration from one cultural environment to another may bring challenges to family values, norms and traditional sources of authority. Let us turn now to consider how we can help the children to cope with these changes and how we can respond to the children's families with greater understanding.

Because of migration, sojourn in another country or death in war, the authority of the traditional head of the family may have been lost and a new authority figure may have to arise.

Rather than lament the absence of the traditional source of support and advice, the parent must take on a greater responsibility in order to give a sense of security to the child.

It will be particularly important to recognise the relative roles and status within the family of the father, mother, grandparents and older relatives. In most cases these roles will be principally determined by the culture, but individual families will vary in the degree to which they follow traditional customs.

If the professional plans to interview the mother in the home, an attempt must be made beforehand to find out whether she will be willing to be interviewed alone or will have others present. This can be an extremely sensitive issue if the professional is male and the parent to be interviewed is the mother or the professional is a woman and the parent the father.

There may be many ways in which the mother's roles in the new cultural environment may be changed. If the mother's role has been expanded by her own modernisation, both she and her family may appreciate her greater empowerment. However, if the change has been thrust upon her through migration or loss, she may suffer from role conflicts and feel bewilderment and culture shock. Helping the mother to obtain more confidence through participation in parent–school activities, or through obtaining further education – especially learning the language in a host country – will assist both mother and child. But the professional must not demand of the mother what is not within her cultural experience or expect her to change to fit in with one's own expectations. Nevertheless, one must beware of stereotyping.

Work in the new culture is another source of expanding the mother's role, but does not always lead to role enhancement if poor working conditions are her lot. Many outworkers who do factory sewing in their own homes may work long hours with little reward and little social contact with others.

In helping the mother's adjustment to her new environment, the child's respect for elders need not be undermined. Depending on the child's age, it can be explained how things change over time, even in the family. The child will be willing to show respect if the parents also convey a sense of respect, but not if the parent does so at the price of losing his or her own authority and autonomy.

Encourage the child to have pride in the family's cultural identity. (More will be said on this topic in Chapter 5.)

Increase your own knowledge of the child's culture. Find out about religious and other taboos, festivals and fasting periods. Respect cultural prohibitions and encourage sharing of festive occasions. For example, the fasting period of Ramadan is extremely significant for Muslims. Young children do not fast but older children take pride in participating. Do not expect children to be as alert as usual during the day; it is a time when all the family come together, when many activities take place at night and all are up before dawn to take the morning meal before sunrise. Check on the different rules for girls and women during this time.

Adapt your teaching styles to accepted cultural styles. Many cultures do not use direct question-and-answer techniques. An oblique style which is less confronting may be needed. This can apply to adults as well as to children.

Many cultures expect the professional to show his or her authority by doing something. Permissive methods will not be effective in an authoritarian or hierarchical style of family culture. You may need to demonstrate to the parent the underlying discipline of the child's treatment when in your care.

Select goals for the child's development which are mutually and culturally acceptable. Discover the expected milestones. For example, in early childhood what is the usual age of weaning or toilet training? What does the parent demand of the child in the balance of study and leisure time? How much experience does the child have with other people, with other family members or with non-members of the family? Does the family want to encourage independence or dependence? Is autonomy or interdependence the mark of a mature person in that culture?

When it is necessary to interview any family member use channels of approach which are culturally acceptable and non-threatening. In many cultures directness of questioning is not acceptable; the matter will only be addressed after courtesies have been exchanged and, probably, after some refreshments are taken. The matter may then be approached by indirect references which are expressed in language designed to save face for all concerned. Prior cultural knowledge is needed to avoid problems.

If the parent does not speak your language, be careful about who is used as an interpreter. Do not use the child as an interpreter, especially in difficult situations. The substance of the discussion may be beyond the child's real understanding, in which case there is a loss of precision as well as a loss of face, or it may involve knowledge which the parent may consider inappropriate for the child to have and so the response will not reflect the true situation. Obtain help from a recognised interpreter service if one is available, otherwise try to use an elder of the culture with proven language skills and integrity. Unfortunately it is often the case that those who have a greater command of other languages are themselves marginal to their own culture.

Use language that is appropriate. When conversing in your own language with those who are less fluent, avoid slang, colloquialisms and idiomatic phrases. These are much more difficult to comprehend than formal terms. Formal language can be friendly while still avoiding unwelcome suggestions of intimacy.

Do not let younger siblings usurp the status of their elder siblings. Often the younger ones have come to the new country at a younger age and have picked up the language more quickly than their older brothers and sisters or their parents. It is tempting, therefore, to turn to the younger child to explain or give a direction meant for the older one. This sends a mixed message to both younger and older siblings and undermines the family structure and relationships within the family.

Above all, respect the cultural values of the child's parents even when they differ from your own. You do not have to agree with them in order to show respect. Insincerity on your part will quickly become transparent, but a genuine effort to understand the child's relationship with the family culture and its expectations for the child will be rewarding in your dealings with the child and with other family members as well.

SUGGESTIONS FOR FURTHER READING

Kağitçibaşi, Ç. (1995). *Family and Human Development across Cultures: A View from the Other Side.* New Jersey: Earlbaum.
Storer, D. (Ed.) (1985). *Ethnic Family Values in Australia.* Sydney: Prentice Hall.

4

SOCIAL INTERACTIONS

In almost all cultures the young child learns the basic skills for effective interactions with others from the close relationships within the family. Beginning with the earliest contact between mother and her baby, the child responds to the social stimuli of eye gaze, sound and touch (Keller & Eibl-Eibesfeldt, 1989). Much has been written about the importance of these early relationships and the differences between Western and non-Western cultures. (See, for example, Keller, Schölmerich & Eibl-Eibesfeldt, 1988; Bornstein, 1990a, 1990b.) In Western cultures the child sleeps alone from an early age and may have a room of its own. In so many other cultures the young child is never separated from another person. In Africa, the child may be carried on the hip or on the back (Munroe & Munroe, 1994; Nsamenang, 1992), in Japan the child does not leave the mother's sight (Doi, 1981), while in many rural cultures the child is carried by the mother or a sibling, many taking turns to hold the child. In this way these children become accustomed to the presence of others as the essential basis of learning their social responsibilities and the source of satisfying social relationships.

As the child's social horizons widen, the number of interactions with others increases, bringing new relationships to be mastered. In this chapter we will be especially concerned with how the child's culture influences the development of social competence. Of particular relevance to the issue is how children interact with other children and adults who may have a different cultural background from their own.

The professional's role is to assist the development of a socially competent and happy child. This means that the child should be helped to maintain good relations with carers and other children as well as with parents. The foundation for tolerance and understanding of other people's way of life, their beliefs and values can begin in quite young children. Thus intolerance and prejudicial beliefs can also be inculcated from an early age. These values do not suddenly appear but begin in the simpler relationships of early childhood.

If children are to grow to adulthood in multicultural societies, the process of learning to live with others who are different has to begin in the way that the child is introduced to the cultures of others. Children bring to their first contacts with others who are different from themselves many of the attitudes of their parents. These attitudes are often expressed to the child in the form of rules and prohibitions, such as 'Don't play with . . ., they're dirty, or not nice', 'Don't eat that funny kind of food', 'Make sure you stay with . . . (a child of the same cultural background)', etc. These instructions may not be fully understood by the child for the fears and underlying cultural values they contain; they only receive them as what their parents have told them is right.

If the professionals and other adults expect the child to relate differently to those children, the child is faced with a dilemma. One solution is to act differently in different situations, obeying the adults who are in control at that place and time. The child might behave as the school wants when at school, but as the parents wish when at home. In the following chapter we will see how this approach can lead to situated identities (Weinreich, 1986) – that is, having different concepts about oneself according to the social context. This strategy can work if the adults never interact and the child is not sensitive to a conflict. The child can also respond in this way if its value development has as yet reached only the stage of norms rather than internalised values (Keats, 1981, 1986). However, this strategy may not be an effective solution in the long term if the conflicting demands cannot be accommodated. In older children the conflict can produce very high levels of anxiety. Acting differently from parental expectations can be seen as deception with accompanying feelings of guilt. These feelings can be exacerbated in the adolescent who wants to mix with other adolescents who may be from backgrounds of which the parents disapprove. We will take up these problems in more detail in Chapter 6.

As professionals who need to come to grips with these issues, perhaps the first step is to examine one's own attitudes and values. These can be conveyed to children in many subtle ways, both verbally and non-verbally. The parents will put their own interpretation upon the child's reporting. However, as was stressed in the previous chapter, there is no substitute for cultural knowledge; understanding the sources of difference does not necessarily mean blind acceptance.

CULTURAL FACTORS IN SOCIAL DEVELOPMENT

In every healthy child there will be a general development in all aspects of social behaviour. From early childhood to adolescence many changes will take place, joint products of the child's own biological maturation and the influences of the social environment in which the child is growing up.

Children's social development in Western cultures has been studied extensively. Piaget, Kagan, Selman, Bandura and Valsiner are some of the most influential theorists. (See 'Suggestions for further reading' at the end of this chapter for useful references to gain access to their ideas and work.) Piaget's approach is essentially cognitive, Kagan's approach is social-developmental, Selman's approach combines cognitive and social concepts, Bandura's approach is based on social learning theory and Valsiner brings a co-constructivist approach.

There is less known in the West about children's social development in non-Western cultures. As many of the children in multicultural societies now come from non-Western backgrounds it is important to know some of the work that has been done. We can draw on research in cross-cultural psychology and by ISSBD and there is also a growing volume of work being carried out in many non-Western countries by indigenous psychologists. For example, many studies have been carried out in Thailand (see Suvannathat *et al.*, 1985) and India (see, for example, Kakar, 1979; Sinha, 1995), and in China the Child Development Centre of China has sponsored much research (e.g. Child Development Centre of China, 1993), as has the Developmental Group of the Institute of Psychology of the Chinese Academy of Sciences. In Japan, Kashiwagi and Azuma are prominent among many; in Turkey, Kagitcibasi leads an active group, and Nsamenang presents a viewpoint from Africa. These are but a few examples of cultures where the social development of children is now being studied from both an indigenous and a cross-cultural approach.

It has been shown in many studies that children from Asian backgrounds are more advanced than children from Western backgrounds in social skills. Cross-cultural comparisons between Japanese, Chinese and American children by Stevenson and his colleagues (Stevenson, Azuma & Hakuta, 1986) and between Chinese and Australian children (Fang & Keats, 1989; Keats & Fang, 1992, 1996) consistently show an earlier development of skills involving social relationships in the Japanese and Chinese than in the American and Australian children. Thai children also have been shown to display earlier development of social perspective-taking skills than was found by Selman's studies in the United States. Studies of the development of aggression by Kornadt *et al.* (1992) show German children to develop the aggression motive earlier and to a greater degree than children from Japanese, Balinese and Acheh (Sumatran) cultures.

A possible explanation for these differences may be found in the collectivist nature of many of the non-Western cultures where the interdependent, relational aspects of development are held to be more important than development of the self by the individual. Western concepts of desirable social development tend to favour the development of individualistic skills, expressed in terms of how the child becomes socially effective as an individual. There is much emphasis on the development of the self, on forming and maintaining an adequate self-concept and encouraging self-esteem. Bandura's social learning theory stresses the development of self-efficacy and the goal of development of the child is the individual's autonomy as an adult.

In collectivist societies such as China, Japan, Turkey, India and many others, the individual is not the main focus. The socially effective adult is one who is a good group member, who honours mutual obligations within the family and develops the social skills necessary for creating and maintaining harmonious relationships with others (Markus & Kitayama, 1991).

Perhaps the most socially collectivist is Japan, where the group adherence begins within the family, then extends to within the age group, then the school and college group, and finally the business group. Group loyalties can demand participation in all aspects of social life, with holidays together, playing together, and even group marriage ceremonies and honeymoons as a group.

Learning social competence means learning how to act in harmony with the group. Hence goals, attitudes and values develop in common accord. They are often given symbolic expression in the wearing of distinctive clothing styles, badges and various other insignia denoting group solidarity.

While those who are perceived by themselves and others as being within the group learn to relate fully to each other, those outside the group will not be granted the same acceptance. Social bonds within groups are stronger in the collectivist cultures than in the more individualistic cultures, but in the individualistic cultures it can be easier to relate to others outside the immediate group because the barriers are weaker. Thus one could expect that children from family-dominated collectivist cultural backgrounds might have difficulty in relating to children and adults from other more individualistic backgrounds. However, within their own cultural group the same children might show little evidence of insecurity.

One of the most important aspects of social development in all cultures is gender role learning. Although cultures differ greatly in what is perceived as appropriate gender role behaviour, research evidence (Williams and Best, 1982) shows that there is also a large amount of agreement. The differences are greatest between modern and traditional cultures and between urban and rural groups within cultures. Traditional cultures make greater role distinctions than modern cultures, and rural people of most cultures make greater distinctions than urban dwellers. These distinctions are maintained most strongly in the middle classes, the well-to-do women having more freedom and the poorer women having to take a greater burden of the work.

Parents begin gender role distinctions at a very early stage in the child's life, and it is not uncommon for parents to prepare themselves confidently during the pregnancy for the child they want, whether it be a boy or a girl, without benefit of amniocentesis. There are many cases of parents treating the child as if it was of the sex they desired when the baby was in fact the opposite. A boy may be dressed as a girl, given dolls to play with, even a girl's name, or, if the child turns out to be a girl and a boy was wanted, dressed as a boy, given a boy's name and treated as a boy. As these cases show, in Western families gender distinctions are introduced into the child's clothing, toys and room furnishings. In almost all cultures boys are expected to be the more active. Girls generally spend more time indoors than boys from the same social background.

These differences are perpetuated as the child grows up, becoming more marked as the child approaches puberty. At this stage the cultural differences become more apparent. In most cultures, and particularly in traditional families, there will be insistence on segregation in social activities. At this stage also the adolescent is likely to show a greater interest in social contacts outside the home, especially with peer groups. When these outside interests show an inclination to include opposite sex peers or peers from another cultural background, families with rigid gender role expectations may find that their admonitions are ignored.

The open resistance which is often written about in Western accounts of adolescents is rare in traditional collectivist families with high cohesion. McDonald (1991) reports that in Australia it is rare for adolescents from such family backgrounds to leave home. The more likely response is to comply, albeit with resentment, restricting their contacts in response to their parents' demands and mixing socially only with people of their own culture. This restriction on choice can reinforce any prejudiced attitudes prevalent in the family. Another strategy is to behave conformingly within the family but mix with others when away.

Yet another response is to adopt behaviour that is even more ideologically culture-bound than the values of the parents. Extremist and fundamentalist movements of all kinds attract young people who use this approach to dealing with cultural differences. Some have a religious basis, others an economic and/or political focus. In some countries these factors combine to produce powerful group motivations. In societies with minority ethnic groups the targets are frequently members of another culture.

Adolescents in this frame of mind are easily attracted by charismatic figures. Such persons can have both supportive and regressive influences on the young person's social development. Indeed, the most powerful figures can exert both at the same time, producing conflicts of values and motivations which are overcome only by blind adherence to the leader's demands.

Also, at this stage, many adolescents from minority ethnic groups become more aware of society's treatment of members of their culture as a minority. When cultural difference is combined with endemic social disadvantage, as in the case of American-Indian and Australian Aborigines, the growing awareness of their disadvantaged position leads to a loss of self-esteem (McInerny, 1990). Apathy and antisocial behaviour are both common.

These young people are particularly vulnerable in situations where there is little prospect of employment and they have little chance of advancing themselves through further education or vocational training. Often their school records have become poorer the further they went in school and they are only too ready to escape, preferably before the age of compulsory schooling is reached. Some, seeking support in their peer group, will join teenage gangs of the same ethnic group and engage in lawlessness, vandalism and substance abuse to give expression to their anger.

In a social climate in which most are not succeeding, those who do have the ability and the wish to may be discouraged from appearing to do better than their contempories. 'Cutting down tall poppies' is a very common phenomenon in many cultures (Feather, 1989). Among Aboriginal people 'big noting' is frowned upon, an attempt to rise above the situation of their peers being seen as a denial of their Aboriginality and moving outside their collectivist group cultural values (Lazarevic, 1992).

In societies which emphasise interdependence within the group rather than the autonomy of the individual, there is a greater emphasis on maintaining harmonious relations than in societies which emphasise the individual rather than the group. In behavioural terms this value may be expressed somewhat differently in different cultures. It has the effect of restricting or controlling the outward expression of emotion, especially anger, and disagreement is often masked by superficial pleasantries. Because it is shameful to fail to maintain harmonious social relations every effort must be made to keep control of oneself and not create situations where others for whom one has respect or with whom one wants to maintain friendly relations will lose control.

The Chinese concepts of 'saving face' and 'losing face' are perhaps the most well known. Ho (1974) discusses the important differences between *lien* and *mien-tzu*. As defined by Hu (1944, cited by Ho, 1974), *lien* involves the confidence of society in one's moral character, and loss of *lien* makes it impossible to function properly within the community. *Mien-tzu* involves reputation and prestige, success and ostentation. The more prominent a person, the more important it is to maintain *mien-tzu*. *Mien-tzu* is lost when the performance falls below the minimum requirements of what would be expected from a person in that position. Loss of *lien* is loss of integrity, and involves a deep sense of shame. The preservation of face is extended to others. Ho (1974, p. 248) states,

> The importance of extending due regard for the face of others can hardly be overemphasised in Chinese social intercourse. To be careful about not hurting someone's face is not simply a matter of being kind or considerate; it functions to avoid conflict, or, more precisely, to avoid confrontation or bringing conflict out into the open. This conflict avoidance is a basic orientation in Chinese social processes rooted in the Confucian model of society based on the maintenance of harmony in interpersonal relations.

Ho notes, however, that a danger inherent in dealing with conflicts on the basis of face saving is that it can lead to confrontation avoidance without a genuine resolution of the conflict. Thus face saving takes precedence over solution to the problem, and when conflicts do erupt into the open they are likely to take a violent form. Ensuring that no shame is brought to the family is frequently used as a deterrent in Chinese child-rearing practices (Ho, 1986; 1994).

To the Japanese also, keeping up smoothness in social relations is essential to harmonious social behaviour. Children are taught that to be a mature and intelligent adult it is necessary to know how to relate socially. Individualists are frowned upon. Ostracism from the group is one of the worst punishments that can be endured. As in Chinese families, fear of bringing shame to the family is used as a deterrent.

The Thai concept of *krengjai* emphasises smoothness and empathy. In a manner somewhat similar to saving face, *krengjai* means to act in a way that supports the other person's self-esteem. Thus it may be difficult for Westerners to interpret the underlying concerns of the ever-smiling, ever-courteous Thai. Training in this social skill is begun from an early age and may certainly account for the superior performance of Thai children in studies of social perspective-taking ability (Vanindananda, 1985) compared with American.

In Java, Indonesia, the values of *hormat*, respect, and *rukun*, maintaining harmonious relations, are taught to children early. These values not only help to maintain social harmony, they also reinforce the hierarchical structure of that society (Mulder, 1992a, 1992b).

In India the training is less explicit, but, as with the cultures mentioned above, the avoidance of direct statement expresses a similar concern with preserving social harmony (Verma, 1995).

Each of these Asian cultures has in common the collectivist group centredness and the avoidance of adversarial confrontations. Maintaining harmonious social relations depends on a respect for status and the empathetic control of emotional expression. The more open, transparent, social style of the Westerner can contrast sharply with the sophisticated conversational ballets in which people of these cultures may engage. Taught as they have been in these behaviours from an early age, by adolescence many of these young people will have acquired the basics of these skills and some will have reached a high level of performance and internalised the norms as values.

In contrast, these styles of social interaction are not considered so important for the Western child to learn. As the brief snapshots in the previous chapter illustrated, there is a greater emphasis on individual personality than on the group. Social skills are taught with the aim of developing self-esteem, and popularity with peers is considered an indication of a socially competent child.

The processes by which these different goals of social development are achieved also vary. However, there are some common methods which can be found in most cultures. Modelling from a role model is used extensively. Direct training by verbal instruction, reward and punishment, indirect training by providing fantasy experiences through games and stories are some of the many methods that can be found in varying forms in most cultures.

DEALING WITH CULTURAL FACTORS IN CHILDREN'S SOCIAL INTERACTIONS

The professional's problems in dealing with social interactions in multicultural situations derive from the diversity of cultural expectations as to what is desirable social behaviour. What one group of parents applauds, another appears to decry; what is praised in one culture is punished in another. Conflicting messages passed on to the child from professionals on the one hand and from parents and other significant persons in the family's culture on the other confuse the child and can create high levels of anxiety.

To avoid these problems and to encourage the child's effective social development, we have to take different approaches depending on the child's age, individual abilities and cultural knowledge. It is also important to take into account the child's place in the family and the family structure and values as described in the previous chapter.

Do not assume that a prohibition is based solely on prejudice. 'Don't mix with those children' may have a basis other than culture or ethnicity. It will be important to find out the basis for the prohibition, be it lack of hygiene, swearing and other undesirable social practices, violence in the home or religious difference. There may be valid reasons for the parents' concern which are not apparent to the child and which the parents may find difficult to explain.

One must also accommodate religious food taboos without causing embarrassment or shame to the child who is different from the mainstream. Being told by the carer or pre-school teacher to eat what is forbidden by the parents can create a terrifying conflict in a sensitive child. If the child obeys the teacher, the parents will be angry and if the child does not eat the food the teacher might single out the child, asking questions which the child does not know how to answer and making the child feel an outcast from the group.

One of the most common problems is whether or not to insist that young Moslem girls should not wear the cover-up clothing and head scarf in a non-Moslem school. It is probably better not to attempt to change the parents' treatment of the child. Ignore the difference as far as possible. When other children ask, explain in simple language, stressing the great variety of clothing styles in the many cultures of the world. Be sure not to exclude the child from the group's activities on the grounds that her clothing will get in the way or that she will stand out too much from the other members of the group. School uniforms in many countries will also present a problem later and some compromises may have to be worked out with the school.

Promotion of harmonious social interactions can begin in the pre-school and child care centre. The young children generally do not understand prejudice and can mix happily together. It is the professional who needs to check his or her own attitudes, and it is in dealing with the parents that these attitudes quickly become apparent. One needs to ask oneself what is being conveyed to the parent by the non-verbal messages as well as by what is said.

In dealing with the child's parents you will want to convey a sense of warmth and friendliness. However, it is often better to be more formal rather than to risk conveying a presumption of intimacy which may be resented. Get to know the norms of social interaction for that culture. For example, do not place your hand on the head of a child of parents who are devout Buddhists as the head is held to be the most sacred part of the body; with Moslem families, do not use your left hand to greet or eat and do not insist that the child does so to conform to the cultures of the other children.

It is important to try to understand what is behind the words in conversing with parents from cultures such as the Chinese, Japanese, Thai or Indonesian who place great emphasis on smoothness in social communication. In interviews do not take everything said at face value or try to go straight to the issue. Take time to establish a good relationship through appropriate courteous exchanges before approaching any issue of concern. The more delicate the subject to be addressed, the more important these courtesies become.

Knowledge of other cultures can be promoted through social events, involving parents wherever possible. However, when children are in day-long child care, it is usually because both parents are at work. It is not then possible to involve either of the parents in social events during the day and in the evenings they may be too tired to make the effort. If a suitable time cannot be found, do not blame the parent for being uncooperative.

Promoting acceptance of people of other cultures through trying different kinds of foods can be both enjoyable and educational: to eat at someone's table is worldwide a sign of
friendship and acceptance. In the pre-school and child care
centre this can be done in the course of the children's daily
meals and by having special days when children of the different cultural groups bring special treats from their culture.
Avoiding foods which are subject to religious taboos is a relatively simple precaution. There are many tempting treats for
young children to sample from cultures other than their own.
Sweets are popular but one needs to be careful with the strong
flavours of foods highly spiced with chilli or garlic, which
need palate training even in their own cultures. Mothers who
cannot come to the centre may be quite happy to provide a
sample of some favourite food from their culture.

Music is another medium with great potential for promoting
enjoyable and supportive social interaction. It also has appeal
to people of all ages. Almost all cultures have a rich heritage of
children's songs and many traditional songs are sung in a number of languages. For example, a popular song book for young
Chinese children is *One Hundred Songs from Around the World*,
which they learn in Chinese or in the foreign language. Among
the most popular are Christmas carols. Young children pick up
the foreign words quite happily, unconcerned about fine differences in pronunciation which might deter adults. Music has
a particularly strong appeal to adolescents and they can be
introduced to other cultures through the popular music scene.
Dance and drama can also be used to widen cultural horizons
in acceptable ways without pressure or heavy handed instruction to which many adolescents react negatively.

For those professionals who work with adolescents the most
frequent problems in social interactions involve relations with
parents and mixing with other young people in the peer
group. These problems often take the form of parents impos-
ing restrictions on the child in keeping with the expectations
of the culture, but the child resenting the constraints which

schoolmates and friends from other cultures do not have to suffer. At this age the parental prohibition, 'Don't mix with those girls or boys', takes on a different meaning. The parents fear that 'bad company' will threaten the traditional values which they have inculcated in the child. Such fears are especially directed to sexual behaviour – a bad reputation or a loss of virginity in girls being most feared. Non-segregated schools are targets for many such concerns.

It has been observed, however, that parental strictness may in fact be greater in the country of immigration than would be the case in the home country (Georgas, 1989; Georgas & Papastyliano, 1994). Many Greeks returning to Greece from living a number of years in Australia have found this to be so. It has been shown also, however, that although the teenage children of immigrant parents want to mix more with their peers from other cultures and take on many of the behaviours and fashions of the others, the important cultural values are highly resistant to change. When these values are soundly based in traditional principles of morality rather than merely in unquestioned traditional practices, parents have little to fear from the wider social interactions of their adolescent children.

SOME SUGGESTIONS FOR FURTHER READING

Bandura, A. (1986). *The Social Foundations of Thought and Action: A Social-Cognitive Theory*. Englewood Cliffs, NJ: Prentice Hall.

Piaget, J. (1932). *The Moral Judgement of the Child*. London: Routledge & Kegan Paul.

Piaget, J. (1981). *Intelligence and Affectivity: Their Relationship during Child Development* (translated and edited by T.A. Brown & C.E. Kaegi). Palo Alto, CA: Annual Reviews Inc.

Selman, R.L. (1980). *The Growth of Interpersonal Understanding*. New York: Academic Press.

Valsiner, J. (1987). *Culture and the Development of Children's Action: A Cultural–Historical Theory of Developmental Psychology*. Chichester: Wiley.

For many contributions on the work of Kagan, see Skolnick, A.S. (1986). *The Psychology of Human Development*. New York: Harcourt Brace Jovanovich.

5

THE DEVELOPMENT OF CONCEPTS OF CULTURAL IDENTITY

In this chapter we consider how children come to understand the meaning of their cultural identity. Cultural identity is that component of the concept of the self which is concerned with one's sense of embeddedness in one's family past, present and future and one's place in the wider cultural milieu.

Cultural identity has its roots in one's ethnic background but encompasses other psychological attributes: it is affective in that it includes feelings; it is perceptual in that it involves the observation of similarities and differences in perceptual cues; and it is cognitive in that it is a concept of what one is. How one feels about what one perceives oneself to be is one's level of self-esteem. The concepts that an adult has about his or her cultural identity can be extremely complex, influenced by many external forces as well as by the person's own thinking. In this chapter we want to consider how children develop their ideas about their own cultural identity and the role that these ideas play in influencing their self-esteem.

To the person who was brought up in an ethnically homogeneous country the possibility that one's cultural identity might differ from one's ethnic identity simply does not arise. Differences which distinguish people socially are put down to such factors as socio-economic class, rural versus urban environment, level of education and individual differences rather than being treated as cultural factors. History might record invasions by foreign conquerors of long ago, but those immigrants of the past have been absorbed long since into the social and cultural fabric. In these circumstances it remains for the curiosity of those who trace their family trees, the academic interest of etymologists concerned with the origins of the words in the language, and the legacies left in the names of villages, towns and cities to suggest the presence of cultural and ethnic differences in identity.

But such an identity consensus is not the case in many countries today where the international movements of people through travel, sojourning, emigration and refugee flight have created ethnically and culturally heterogeneous populations. For the children of these populations the possible conflict between ethnic and cultural identity is no mere theoretical abstraction.

To understand the problems involved in the development of the sense of cultural identity we need to begin by considering what is involved in the concept. Two theoretical approaches will be found helpful: first, the distinctions between ethnic and cultural identity made by Thomas (1986) which were introduced in Chapter 1, and, second, the theoretical conceptualisation of situated identities as set down by Weinreich and his colleagues (Weinreich, 1986; Weinreich, Kelly & Maja, 1987).

Developmentally the process by which these concepts are acquired is a gradual one, bringing into play both the development of cognitive abilities in the child and the influence of social forces. An interesting case showing the role of cognitive development was demonstrated by Piaget and Weil (1951). They asked Swiss children from Geneva questions about the nature of foreigners and their ideas about the homeland. The younger children could not understand that one could be Swiss and Genevese at the same time, but by 11 to 12 years the concept was generally understood. To questions about the concept of being a foreigner, children of about 7 to 8 years denied that they could ever be a foreigner and thought that a foreign child would choose Switzerland as a homeland if that child had been born without a homeland. The actual knowledge of children of another culture was minimal, and, in the younger children especially, their opinions were egocentric.

Role models from within the family provide potent social influences upon the child in its early years, but, as we have seen in the previous chapter, as the child grows the number of role model referents increases and their relative potency may also change. We need, therefore, to place the development of the concept of cultural identity in the general framework of the child's social, cognitive and emotional development. Valsiner's (1995) co-constructivist approach referred to in the previous chapter allows for this intimate interplay between the child and the significant other. The role model referent and the child each work together to construct the child's world. The messages which are conveyed about the child's culture may be both verbal and non-verbal, expressed in action as often as in verbal instructions.

The concept of ethnic identity as used here and referred to in Chapter 1 takes into account both its genetic and its subjective basis. Many attributes of an ethnic group are cultural in their nature and hence the genetic component is often downplayed. It is also true that cultural differences within ethnic groups are often ignored in ethnically based categorisations. Thomas's (1986) studies in New Zealand with Pakeha (i.e. European) children and children of Maori descent show that this tendency to use simple ethnic categorisations can obscure important cultural differences. Thomas points out that a common categorisation used in New Zealand is 'Maori', 'Pakeha' and 'Other'. However, in studies with children Thomas used a fourfold categorisation allowing children to identify themselves as being Pakeha, Mostly Pakeha, Mostly Maori or Maori. This fourfold ethnic identification brought out differences in cultural identity in the Maori groups. A Test of Maori Knowledge was administered. This 40-item test contained items about Maori culture and language and the results were related to performance on standardised school achievement tests in mathematics and language. On the Test of Maori Knowledge, scores for the Pakeha children were the lowest, second lowest were the scores of the Mostly Pakeha group, the Mostly Maori group were second highest and the Maori group the highest. These results were related to the achievement scores by grouping the ethnic Maori children into those who scored at better than chance level on the Test of Maori Knowledge and those who showed little or no knowledge of Maori culture. It was found that ethnic Maori children who scored in the high cultural knowledge group also scored higher on the achievement tests. Thomas concluded that the results emphasised the need to distinguish ethnicity from culture and refuted the notion that being culturally Maori was educationally disadvantageous.

A somewhat different approach to examining cultural identity has been taken by Weinreich (Weinreich, 1986; Weinreich, Kelly & Maja, 1987) in his conceptualisation and measurement of identity structure. Central to Weinreich's theory is the recognition that people will engage in different identity states when in different social contexts. A familiar example is the businessman who can be a terrifying boss in the office but a henpecked husband at home. In the case of people from cultural minorities, it can be observed that they may behave very differently when with their own people from how they behave in social contexts with those of the majority culture. Weinreich's approach considers that such differences in behaviour represent differences in how people construe themselves in those situations and thus present different facets of their complex sense of identity.

Weinreich acknowledges the effects of categorisation by others but argues that the person is actively engaged in identity formation, i.e. in 'complex amalgamations of partial identifications with significant others and across social boundaries within and beyond the family' (Weinreich, Kelly & Maja, 1987). Weinreich makes a clear distinction between 'empathic identification' and 'idealistic identification', the former referring to the recognition of shared qualities with another, which could be good or bad, and the latter referring to role model identification, the desire to be like another who is admired. 'Idealistic identification' is also contrasted with 'contra-identification', in which 'an individual dissociates oneself from another'. 'Conflict identification' is defined as a function of the extent of one's empathetic identification with another and the wish to dissociate oneself from the characteristics of that other. This definition implies, therefore, that a person can have empathetic identification at the same time as having contra-identification with another.

That these differing psychological states may be invoked by different social situations does not necessarily mean that a person with differing identification construals will always experience an unstable sense of the self. People may negotiate within the social context in which they operate at a particular time. Moreover, the total context of past, present and future has to be considered. 'Situated identity' is therefore defined as 'that part of the totality of one's self construal in which how one construes oneself in the situated present expresses the continuity between how one was in the past and how one construes oneself as one aspires to be in the future' (Weinreich, Kelly & Maja, 1987, p. 322). Hence conflict identification may be higher in one context than another, bringing out what appears to be 'aberrant' behaviour.

Weinreich and his colleagues have carried out many empirical studies using these concepts. The social contexts and subjects in these studies have included adolescents and adults and a number of ethnic and cultural groups. The concept of situated identities is operationalised by means of his Identity Structure Analysis. The instrument designed for the analysis is similar to the repertory grid technique (Kelly, 1955) with 'self' represented by various facets of the self-image, myself 'as I am now' and myself 'as I am within other social contexts', such as with people of other cultural backgrounds and with significant others (termed 'entities'). A sophisticated computer program (IDEX) was developed to deal with both individual (IDEX-IDIO) and group (IDEX-NOM) data.

One study reported by Weinreich, Kelly & Maja (1987) is of particular relevance for the role of culture in identity formation. In this study, black South African youths' self-identification in three social contexts was compared: as now (i.e. in their natural social context), when with the English, and when with the Afrikaners. Within the Afrikaner social context they tended to identify empathetically with the Afrikaner leadership, but showed highly conflicted and vulnerable identities, in most cases revealing an identity crisis. This was especially the case with the urban youth. Weinreich, Kelly & Maja (1987, pp. 332–333) remark:

> It is quite apparent from the empirical findings that, situated within Afrikanerdom, they do not only find little scope for implementing their aspirations, but they also behave in many respects in ways they do not wish. Within this context they are thoroughly demoralised and their vulnerable identity states are ones from which they would be unable to assert themselves in terms of their identity aspirations.

With the English there was moderately high empathetic identification but not the conflicted identity states that were revealed within the Afrikaner context. In their own 'natural' identity states there were close empathetic identifications with their families and friends and their own ethnic group, there was little evidence of conflicted or vulnerable identities. It would be interesting to examine whether the subsequent political changes have led to any changes in these concepts of cultural identity in black South African youth.

It is clear the Weinreich's approach can deal with both ethnic and cultural identity, and is able to account for apparently contradictory attitudes and behaviours of many young people whose sense of cultural identity is not comfortably integrated in their 'self' concept. When the cultural contexts in which they must behave present differing demands it could be expected that they might experience vulnerable situated identity states similar to those of the African youths in the foregoing example. As an empirical method it can be applied to adults or children as young as 9 years. The actual content of the items can be adapted for particular situations and persons.

Although not specifically expressed in terms of the development of cultural identity in children, the distinction presented by Markus and Kitayama (1991) in their analysis of the contrast between independent and interdependent self-construal is also relevant. Markus and Kitayama have shown how cognitive, attitudinal and emotional components of the construal of the self are influenced by whether the child is brought up in cultures in which the dominant values foster interdependence more than independence. In the more interdependent construal of the self we could expect that cultural identity would be influenced more by interdependent relationships with members of the same cultural group than would be the case for individuals who were brought up to develop a more independent construal of the self.

Neither Weinreich's nor Markus and Kitayama's analysis directly addresses the question of how the conceptualisation of self-construal relates to how the child develops concepts of cultural identity. When does the sense of cultural identity become part of a child's self-construal? How do children learn what they are, their empathetic identification, what they would like to be, their ideal identification, and what is the difference between what they are and what they want to identify with, the conflict identification? Why do they behave differently in different contexts so that others construe their cultural identification differently from the way they themselves do? At what age do they become aware of such differences?

Much of the research work addressing these and similar questions has been done with North American children, mainly Negro, Mexican-American and white children in the United States and Native Indian and white children in Canada. One of the best-known methods has been the use of dolls of contrasting skin colour and ethnic features. This method was pioneered by Clark and Clark (1939, 1947) and has been used in many studies using many different cultural groups. The children are asked questions such as 'Which is the nicest?', 'Which one would you like most?', etc. In these studies it was frequently found that the black children preferred the white dolls, even identifying with them or saying that the black dolls were 'bad' and the white dolls 'nice'.

It should be pointed out that in these studies the researchers did not distinguish between ethnicity and cultural identity, being more concerned with the development of prejudicial attitudes than with the development of concepts of the self. The identity questions appeared almost as an aside in the question, 'Which doll is more like you?' Young children of 4 years of age frequently made errors but these were seldom found in children of 8 years and older. In an extensive review of studies of the development of ethnic attitudes, Aboud and Skerry (1984) found the results to be very mixed. They were critical of the methods on the grounds of lack of demonstrable validity and reliability, the doll stimulus persons did not represent the ethnic group appropriately, and the forced choice responses were too simplistic, not allowing for many possible variations in the intensity of children's attitudes. Because dolls have so many meanings for young children, Aboud and Skerry recommended the use of pictures rather than dolls.

Blue, Corenblum and Annis (1987), in two related studies with Native Indian and white Canadian children, used carefully constructed pictures with ethnic features instead of dolls. In the first of these two studies there were 83 Native Indian children from kindergarten and grade 1 classes in a Native Indian school. The sample was extended in the second study to 230 children drawn from kindergarten, grade 1, grade 2 and grade 4, and including the 83 from the former study. There were also some changes in the method. In the second study the Native Indian children were drawn from an isolated Indian reserve in Manitoba and were tested by native speakers in their own language. Racial preference, labelling accuracy and self-identification were measured, and scores on the Wechsler Intelligence Scale for Children and measures of health were also obtained.

In the first study the Native Indian children behaved in the same way as had been found for black children in previous research, showing a strong bias for the white child in the picture on the preference question. However, this bias was not so pronounced when the children in the second study were tested in their own language.

The developmental aspect was brought out more clearly in the second study. The results showed a developmental trend in the accuracy of labelling the white or Native child in the picture but there was no similar trend in preference or self-identification. Over 80% of the children chose a white child in response to the racial preference questions. An interesting finding was that 75% chose the white child as looking like themselves. Although they could identify and label the white child in the picture correctly, they did not apply the same reasoning to themselves. Another finding was a difference between boys and girls in grades 2 and 4 in self-identification accuracy and preference. The boys were more accurate in identification and more likely to prefer the Native picture; there was also a greater discrepancy between identification and preference in the girls than the boys.

Another method used is a children's version of the 20 Statements Test in which the child has to complete twenty sentences each beginning with 'I am . . .'. This method is suited to older children, but is subject to response bias. There are also likely to be cultural style differences in responding to this type of questionnaire as cultures vary in the willingness to disclose personal feelings.

Rutherford (1993) used a jigsaw puzzle task as stimulus materials in his study of the development of concepts of cultural identity in Thai and Australian children. The children were shown the pieces and were told they could put them together to make a face. The pieces varied in skin colour, hair colour, and colour and shape of the eyes. When put together without error the faces could be either European or Asian in appearance. The children were 5, 9 and 11 years of age. The youngest children could not put the pieces together in consistent combinations, but this ability increased with age so that in the older groups no errors were made and the children understood the basis for their responses.

Another approach is to consider the development of one's concept of cultural identity as an aspect of the development of values (Keats, 1981, 1986). As the child's understanding increases with age, there is a greater understanding of who one is and how this identity is embedded in one's culture. However, these ideas are ill-formed at first, and their development is influence by the attitudes of significant others.

Although these researchers have adopted somewhat different approaches, certain features that emerge clearly from their work have much relevance for understanding how children develop concepts of their own and others' cultural identity. Unfortunately, however, there is often a lack of precise definition in how researchers have used the terms 'ethnic', 'cultural' and 'racial', and this has to be borne in mind when interpreting their findings.

Aboud and Skerry (1984) proposed three stages of development in regard to ethnic attitudes which also have some relevance for the development of concepts of cultural identity. In the first stage the child is mainly concerned with self-identification and self-evaluation. Other group members are not identified in ethnic terms but only as being different from oneself. In the second stage the child is mainly concerned with being a group member and other group members are seen only as belonging to another group. There is an emphasis on between-group differences and similarities and social rules which determine how to react to members of other groups. In the third stage there is again an emphasis on oneself and individuals but the child's perspective has become more differentiated, with reactions to others based on individuals rather than on his or her group membership. Aboud and Skerry point out that not all people achieve this third stage. The process of development of differentiation is seen as the key to whether prejudicial ethnic attitudes will develop. There is a developmental shift from affective to perceptual to cognitive forms of differentiation. Less prejudiced attitudes will involve an emphasis on perceptual and cognitive over affective differentiation. These processes are also consistent with the development of values as proposed by Keats (1981, 1986).

DEALING WITH THE CHILD

So far the issues have been presented at a somewhat abstract level. Let us turn now to some practical considerations for the professional. The professional's task is how to make use of these ideas so that the child's developing concepts about his or her own cultural identity can be fostered in ways which are supportive and provide a firm foundation for the child's future development and adult socio-cultural roles. Here we consider how children's feelings about their cultural identity affect their self-esteem.

In Weinreich, Kelly & Maja's idea of situated identities we have a conceptualisation which can be applied to young children as well as to adolescents and adults. We can see from this idea how a young child could behave differently in different social contexts but not find this a problem of conflict in self-identification, whereas in adolescence the difference between empathetic identification and idealistic identification may become more apparent and lead to contra-identification and conflict identification. We can also see how these processes might work out in children from minority cultural backgrounds, and how contra-identification and conflict identification could be reflected in lower self-esteem.

Context differences of relevance include how the child and the parent perceive their cultural identity. The parent may use situated identities derived mainly or solely from the background of the minority culture, whereas the situated identities of the adolescent son or daughter derive from the different social contexts of the peer group and the school in the minority culture. Weinreich, Kelly & Maja's study of the black African high school students showed this very clearly.

When the child from a minority ethnic group joins with family members in their ethnic group activities such as weddings, ethnic club social evenings, church attendance, etc., the dominant situated identity of the child will be compatible with the cultural identity of the ethnic group. However, when the child is with members of the majority group, this identity will give way to a cultural identity which is influenced by other identifications which may be empathetic or idealistic.

In the case of the child who is not fully accepted by the majority, the situation could be one of conflict identification, in which the child has both the desire to identify empathetically with members of the other group but at the same time wishes to dissociate from them. Moreover, these conflicting identity feelings may also be experienced by the child's parents who convey contradictory messages to the child both directly and in their own behaviour.

When these feelings of identification are applied to culturally related norms, values and behaviour, the potential for affecting self-esteem is very great. When the discrepancy between empathetic and idealistic identifications is great, and when conflict identifications involve competing cultural norms and values, the child has to try to find some accommodation among them. Most manage to do this, but others lose self-esteem because the expectations of the significant others on either side cannot be satisfied.

Encouraging acceptance of the child's cultural roots by the child and by others is a first step. This may also involve showing greater respect for the child's parents. Pride in cultural heritage can be encouraged in many ways which stress the positive attributes of the child's culture.

Because of their different experiences it is quite likely that the child may have different concepts of his or her own cultural identity from his or her parents' concepts. But because parents remain the most important significant others for children in most cultures, a loss of pride in the parental culture is likely to threaten self-esteem. However, it has to be recognised that not all parents are loving and supportive and it is a short step from observing this shortcoming to associating their failure to give the needed emotional support with the values of their cultural background. It may be necessary to help the child avoid this damaging situation.

This problem can be illustrated by the following hypothetical case. The father of a 12-year-old girl from a socially disadvantaged ethnic minority is imprisoned for a minor crime because he is unable to pay the fine. The mother becomes aggressive after a drinking bout and is also taken into custody. Meanwhile the child is removed from the family home and placed in an institution. Here the majority of inmates are of the same ethnic background. The child concludes that there is little hope for people of their background, and blames the culture rather than the parents for the situation. Knowing that her friends at school will no longer want to know her, and that she will be unable to keep up her school work in the institution, she quickly has to succumb to the 'rules' and falls into deep depression. 'If I were . . ., this would not have happened to me' is a common reaction.

The difference between ethnicity and cultural identity needs to be kept in mind and stereotyped judgements about cultural differences on the basis of ethnicity should be avoided. Skin colour and facial characteristics are frequently used indicators of ethnicity, but are unreliable indicators of cultural identity. Be particularly wary of judgements based on external features such as dress. Names, too, can be misleading.

Keep in mind that, for the growing child, coming to the full realisation of one's cultural identity is a gradual process, involving developing cognitive abilities and widening social experiences. Do not expect that young children will have a complete understanding of their own or others' ethnic or cultural identity.

Try to help the child to understand and accept the idea of difference, both individual and cultural. Keep in mind that people within one ethnic categorisation can be very different from each other.

The concept of situated identities can be a very useful one to help the child avoid stressful conflicting identifications. Mixed cultural identities need not necessarily lead to conflict but may be seen as more interesting because of their greater complexity. If the professional who deals with the child takes this view of cultural identity, it will be possible to encourage the development of the same concepts in the growing child, and consequent positive feelings of self worth.

SUGGESTIONS FOR FURTHER READING

George, D.M. & Hoppe, R.A. (1979). Racial identification, preference, and self-concept. *Journal of Cross-Cultural Psychology*, **10**, 85–100.

Phinney, J.S., DuPont, S., Epinosa, C., Revill, J. & Sanders, K. (1994). Ethnic identity and American identification among ethnic minority youths. In A.-M. Bouvy, F.J.R. van de Vijver, P. Boski & P. Schmitz (Eds), *Journeys in Cross-Cultural Psychology*. Amsterdam: Swets & Zeitlinger, pp. 167–183.

6

CULTURAL FACTORS IN CHILDREN'S MOTIVATIONS AND ANXIETIES

Almost all children have worries at some time. In earlier chapters we have been considering some of the main sources of those worries, especially the ways in which children are influenced by family expectations and the social demands of peers and significant others. When we add in, on the one hand, the effects of the child's own individual temperament and, on the other, the child's developing sense of his or her own cultural identity, we can appreciate how daunting the complexity of the child's social psychological world can be. Trying to respond to the competing demands of parents, school and friends is enough to bring about a high degree of uncertainty in most children in any culture, and high levels of anxiety in sensitive children who find themselves in new or different cultural environments should not be unexpected.

When such uncertainties are not resolved, the child's development is adversely affected in many ways. That is not to say that conflict and uncertainty are in themselves entirely negative in their effects. Indeed, both social and cognitive growth require some degree of conflict resolution for development to a further stage to be achieved. It is when the conflict cannot be overcome by means of the child's own ability that anxiety mounts. This may not be because the child lacks either the motivation or the cognitive ability to solve the problem, but because the solution is not in the child's hands. Such is the case when the source of the conflict lies in cultural rather than individual factors. The child may or may not recognise that cultural factors are the source of the problems, but if the child does recognise them the frustration arising from the knowledge that the child cannot change them will cause a high level of anxiety.

To adults some of the things which worry children may seem trivial, but no problem is trivial to the person who wants to solve it but does not have the capacity or the resources to do so. The child's anxiety will only be exacerbated by adults whose response is to minimise the importance of the problem and shrug off the child's concerns. A complication is that both the recognition and the expression of a person's worries and anxieties may be more socially acceptable in some cultures than in others.

Nevertheless, there are some problems which appear to be universal in the growing child. Studies of adolescents' concerns and anxieties have been carried out in many cultures, although those with a cross-cultural methodology are few. In an extensive seventeen nation study of perceived problems and coping strategies, Gibson *et al.* (1991) used open-ended questionnaires with samples of young adolescents and young adults in Australia, Brazil, Canada, Greece, Hong Kong, India, Israel, Japan, Kuwait, the Netherlands, Philippines, Puerto Rico, Soviet Russia, Tanzania, Turkey, the United States and Venezuela. The subjects were classified into three categories of social advantage: advantaged, disadvantaged and disadvantaged/extreme poverty. The Soviet Russian sample was treated separately as it did not fit easily into any of the three categories of advantage, and, in view of the extreme poverty prevalent in some of the countries, allowances were also made for local cultural differences in the basis and distribution of disadvantage.

The extensive content analysis identified thirteen categories of problems mentioned: extreme poverty, war, catastrophe, material desires, family issues, schooling issues, personal identity and self-concept, sexuality, courtship and dating, interpersonal and socialisation issues, emotions and feelings, self-fulfilment, and altruism.

Differences were found on the basis of age and degree of disadvantage but on the perception of problems there was much disagreement. For the total sample of over three thousand adolescents and youth, family, schooling and personal identity/self-concept were the three most frequently cited categories of problems, together accounting for more than 70% of all the responses and for most countries. War, catastrophe and self-fulfilment were cited least often, in that order. In the family category the most frequently cited was domestic quarrelling; in the schooling category the most frequent were academic failure and academic achievement; in the personal identity/self-concept category the most frequent were problems relating to growing up and self-confidence.

Apart from the high ranking given to altruism by the Soviet Russian respondents, the greatest difference was between the extremely disadvantaged poverty group and the advantaged and disadvantaged groups. For the extremely disadvantaged group material issues and problems of extreme poverty were highest after family, schooling and personal identity/self concept issues, whereas material issues and extreme poverty were not high for the other two groups. Concerns about emotions and feelings were not high among the extremely disadvantaged but moderately high in the other three groups. The low ranking of war and catastrophe was common to all groups.

For coping strategies individual problem solving was the most frequent for all groups. There was much less difference in the rankings of these categories than in the citing of problems.

Gender differences were found in very few categories and were of not more than three rank positions. Material desires was ranked sixth by males and ninth by females in the advantaged group; courtship/dating was ranked seventh by Russian females and tenth by Russian males; and fifth by females and eighth by males in the advantaged group.

Differences among countries appeared on particular categories. For example, the Soviet Russian responses were high on altruism as a problem but extreme poverty was not a problem; Japanese were extremely high on school problems but low on family problems; Hong Kong responses were similar to the Japanese; the Philippines was highest on material desires, with Tanzania next highest; Tanzania and Venezuela were highest on poverty; Tanzania was also highest on sexuality; Australia and the United States were also relatively high on schooling issues, but no ethnic breakdowns were given for these two countries.

For the analysis of coping strategies, nine categories of responses were elicited: seek/give assurance, interpersonal, individual problem solving, stress management, crying, religious response, resignation, disengage from the problem, and antisocial response. There was much less difference in the rankings of these categories than in the citing of problems. Individual problem solving was the most frequent for all four groups, followed by seek/give assurance, interpersonal strategies and disengaging from the problem. Antisocial, crying and religious responses were the least frequently cited. The only notable difference among the groups was in the Soviet Russian group's low frequency given to seek/give assurance, which was ranked sixth compared with second and third by the other groups. Overall, these results show a surprising degree of agreement among these young people.

Although carried out with great care in the methodology, the rankings nevertheless may not do full justice to the richness of the data. Because of the need to collapse categories, the category descriptions may contain contradictory components. One such example is the category of seek/give assurance which could imply either asking for help or giving help to others. The family issues category is also very wide in its range. Another is the coping strategy of problem solving, under which many different ways of reacting may be subsumed. There is also the problem of social response bias which may differentially affect responses in different cultures. One would hardly expect many of those who use antisocial coping strategies to admit to this type of behaviour or even agree to participate in the study. Moreover, the total number would not be high in the most honest of groups. However, the study was planned to continue and further work may unravel these anomalies.

At the younger age levels there appear to be no similar studies ranging across a large number of cultures, so inferences have to be drawn from various studies within cultures. There is also some evidence from countries with multicultural populations or ethnic minorities. For example, in Malaysia studies by Chiam (1984), which show some contrasts between Malay and Chinese children, some of the concerns of Malay children differ from the Chinese more in degree than in content. In Singapore there is extensive evidence of high levels of anxiety related to school issues, particularly for the Chinese. Many of these concerns can be traced to the examination system and the system of streaming into academic, technical and other groups from an early age. Anxieties about these issues become more pronounced at the high school level (Crystal *et al.*, 1994).

Evidence from Japan (Kashiwagi, 1986) also supports the Gibson *et al.* (1991) findings of high levels of anxiety related to school issues. As in Singapore, this concern begins very early and can be traced to the highly selective examination system and the status differences in universities, the influence of which reaches down into the elementary school level and can determine the person's lifestyle and future employment. The increase in unemployment in Japan now makes the situation more stressful as security of tenure in jobs is no longer guaranteed.

Singaporean, Chinese and Japanese children and adolescents are found in many countries, in ethnic minorities of long standing, as sojourners and as overseas students in schools and universities. These young people share a common cultural heritage which has a strong emphasis on learning. Learning is seen as a way of improving one's own social status, but from the child's viewpoint good performance in school is the most direct and satisfying way of pleasing one's parents. The traditional viewpoint in both the Chinese and Japanese cultures is that every child can learn. Successful learning brings as much honour to the family as to the child. The prospect of pleasing the family is therefore the greatest motivation and the prospect of failure to achieve school success the greatest source of anxiety, as failure involves not only shame in the child but loss of face for the whole family.

The desire to please one's parents also exerts a powerful control over moral and social behaviour in these children. Ho's discussion in Chapter 4, on the meaning of face and its effects in the use of shame as a deterrent, shows how the Chinese child's anxieties can develop when parents are not pleased. This applies to social and interpersonal relationships as well as school performance, so in most cases there is also strict moral control.

Another aspect of the effect of the motivation to please parents is the case of the child attempting to protect the parent. Over-concern for the parent may create a high level of anxiety in the child, especially when the child is unsuccessful in these efforts. The parent may be suffering from an illness, or, as an immigrant, be having difficulties with the new environment, or be an embarrassment in his or her lack of language skills. A younger child may not realise the source of the anxiety, but an adolescent may be painfully conscious of the problem and suffer the more because it cannot be brought to the surface.

As we saw in the previous chapter, as the child begins to understand its cultural identity it may also begin to realise that what the parents want the child to be is not the same as the child's idea of his or her cultural self. This realisation can become a dilemma for some children of immigrant parents when there is strong pressure from the parents and senior family members to conform to the norms of the parental culture and, at the same time, equally strong pressure for the child to behave like his or her fellow pupils at school or local neighbourhood friends.

In this situation the child may feel that whatever he or she does, it is sure to be wrong. This can be a paralysing situation: fear of the ridicule of one's peers can be a driving motivation to defy one's parents, but it can lead to guilt feelings in the child and anger in the parents. Imposition of stricter rules and punishments which often follow are frequent reactions of the parents but only exacerbate the problem.

As we saw in Chapter 4, many cultures are particularly concerned about sexual propriety and purity in the behaviour of girls. Such prohibitions against social mixing of adolescent boys and girls after puberty can cause much anxiety when the family moves into a more permissive cultural environment. Dating between boys and girls is unknown in traditional Hindu and Moslem families, and in many cultures mixed parties are strictly supervised and very little cross-gender socialising may occur. Their lack of sexual knowledge may also make girls from these traditional backgrounds particularly vulnerable. Unwanted pregnancies are rare, but when they do occur they cause far more disgrace than in more permissive cultures. A not uncommon situation is that the boys have been given more encouragement in sexual development and the girl does not have the ability to respond to the boy's social advances in a comfortable, friendly way.

For the child from a disadvantaged minority, coming to understand one's cultural identity may also lead to the realisation that one's culture is not held in high regard by others in the society. Feeling the sting of prejudice and discrimination can be very painful, especially when the full realisation suddenly becomes clear for the first time. Ostracism often occurs as the mainstream children take on the attitudes of their parents and the dominant cultural views.

What are the child's possible responses? They can range from aggression, apathy and denial to enhanced motivation to compete, as in the following reactions.

- *Sullen dejection and loss of will to succeed.* 'I'll never get on, so what's the use of trying?'
- *Acting out: direct or indirect.* 'I'll pay them back'; or aggression against an inanimate object associated with the persons seen as belonging to the oppressors, e.g. knocking down their fence, painting graffiti on their fence; or seemingly senseless acts of vandalism or aggression against an innocent victim.
- *Rejection of own culture.* Takes up the norms, fashions, etc., of the culture of the majority and rejects all things from one's own.
- *Denial.* 'I'm really the same as them, there's no difference between us.' Refuses to see differences or accept those which are obvious.
- *Unrealistic, idealistic identification with one's own culture.* May exaggerate its virtues and deny any faults. Sees the past history of the culture through rose-coloured glasses.
- *Heightened motivation to achieve.* 'I'll show them I can do even better than they can.'
- *Displacement.* Leaves the field. May leave school and join others as unemployed, take up a sport in which their culture has had representatives, even if not held in high general regard, e.g. travelling boxing troupes.

Which of these strategies the child will adopt will depend on the support that is given by parents and family members, by the child's peer group and by the professionals who work with the child and the family. Another relevant issue is whether the child or adolescent is one of a large group from the same cultural background or not. Where numbers are sufficient, teenage gangs from disadvantaged minorities can easily develop. Nor can a simple single reaction be expected, but combinations of the above with varying weight given to each element and fluctuations vacillating from one to another from time to time. We can also expect a high level of anxiety as the child works through the problem.

For example, if a child begins with motivations to achieve a higher level of performance than others but finds in practice that he does not, he may drop back into sullen dejection followed by an episode of acting out. As neither of these strategies achieves the twin goals of doing better than the others and pleasing his parents, the child's situation does not improve. If the child successfully displaces to a field approved of in his own culture, but not in that of the majority, his self-esteem may increase but his competency in the field he leaves may in fact decrease and hostility against him increase.

Not all cultures encourage the free expression of a person's personal anxieties. Where the social skills of maintaining harmonious social relations are stressed, an external appearance of calm is required, as is the case with Japanese, Chinese and Thai cultures, and neither verbal nor facial expression may be a reliable guide to what the child is feeling. In the British culture the 'stiff upper lip' is still admired by many, and 'boys don't cry' is still used to discourage a more open display of emotion in males. On the other hand, the more volatile expression of emotion in Latin, West Indian and Afro-American cultures provides a strong contrast. In young children emotional ups and downs may be expressed in crying, temper tantrums and clinging to adult caregivers. The professional may fail to observe the presence of emotional stress in the less demonstrative child, but seldom will fail to react to the volatile style which may seem to express a greater need.

Many normal children suffer from vivid and terrifying fears at some time. In many cases these have a cultural basis. Bogeymen, witches and bad men who might carry off the naughty child are the stuff of the disciplinary threats in many cultures. Children who have experienced wars and refugee camps, who have accompanied their families on dangerous journeys of escape from their original countries, and who have been in road accidents and natural disasters or have lost a close relative through death, all are vulnerable to recurrent fears. Many of these experiences leave scars which do not fully heal. Such highly anxious children need special care, but this is a topic beyond the scope of this book.

In many of those cultures which use bogeymen and the like as deterrents, the normal child does not necessarily suffer from excessive fears. One reason for this is that the child does not have to suffer from internalised feelings of guilt but has only to change its behaviour. The more common fears of children arise from physical threats such as bullying by other bigger and stronger children. Another source of fear is having a strange and new experience which involves some inherent danger. For example, the first occasion of swimming in the ocean can be a source of great terror to a child who has not been brought up in a seaboard environment.

DEALING WITH CHILDREN'S ANXIETIES

One of the first and most important tasks for the professional in dealing with children's anxieties is to recognise them for what they are. What does the child's behaviour reveal? What does it hide? Next is the question of what to do about it. We can ask whether the anxiety stems from problems in the child's relationships with parents, peers or authority figures, from the child's achievement motivations and failures to meet their own (and their parents') expectations, from the child's individual temperamental style reflected in the reactions of others towards the child, from inner conflicts generated by the realisation of the implications of minority status, or from fears rational and irrational. Then comes the question of where and how to begin the complex task of helping the child to overcome these anxieties in ways which will lead to healthy growth. The practical issue is whether to try to change the child's behaviour or his or her attitudes.

Attitude change can be brought about in a number of ways. Kelman (1961) was one of the first to show that an enforced change in behaviour can lead to the internalisation of attitudes associated with the new behaviour. Through the intermediate stage of conformity, the person comes to accept the new behaviour in a stage of identification, and from identification of oneself with the new behaviour and what is associated with it, the next step is a shift to internalising the attitude so that it is regarded as the right one. This process is akin to the shift in values development from the acceptance of norms enforced by significant others to the internalisation of those norms as correct beliefs or behaviour.

This approach is similar to, but not exactly the same as, that of Bandura's (1986) cognitive-behaviourist social learning theory. In Bandura's approach the acquisition of self-efficacy is stressed. Modelling is an integral component in promoting the development of self-efficacy. The parents' and significant other adults' own attitudes and behaviour are the primary sources of such models. One source of a child's anxiety is that the powerful models provided by parents and other adults may present conflicting pictures.

It is apparent that behavioural methods will be effective with younger children. However, with older adolescents the cognitive aspects become more influential. Many anxieties of adolescents arise from their ability to contemplate in their minds the fearful consequences of failure or the disastrous loss of peer acceptance in social relationships. In their anxious state these dire consequences can easily become exaggerated.

To assist the child's development of a sense of self-worth, other supportive behaviour is also needed. Warm and loving relationships showing acceptance of the child are important for children of all cultures. These needs are no less those of adolescents than of younger children, and even more the needs of those children who find themselves in an alien cultural environment.

Indicators that the child is experiencing anxiety will vary with age, gender and culture. The professional may notice any of the following behaviours, especially if the behaviour is not typical of the child's usual temperamental style.

- Unwillingness to try something new.
- Unwillingness to face a challenging task, especially if the task is not a new one.
- General fearfulness of risk taking.
- Fiddling with hair and or clothing.
- Biting fingernails.
- Rocking in the one place.
- Compulsive movement of legs or feet under the table.
- Tearing up paper into shreds.
- Loss of appetite.
- Over-eating, eats when things go wrong.
- Enuresis or loss of bowel control.
- Easy to come to tears.
- Unexpected disobedience on trivial issues.
- Shuts self in room with loud music to repel entry by adults.
- Does not respond to parents' calls.
- Daydreaming, spends a long time doing nothing.
- Spends a long time on tasks but does not complete them.
- Is never satisfied with product.
- Cannot stick to a given task.
- Sleeps more than the healthy requirement for the child's age.
- Too tidy.
- Too clean.
- Too good.

- Poor physical tone.
- Lacks friends, especially friends in own age group.
- Averts eyes from others in cultures which encourage eye contact.
- Uses direct gaze in cultures in which direct gaze is confronting.
- Vacillates between own and another culture but is not fully accepted in either.
- Seeks hedonistic excitement, drugs, smoking, drinking.
- Non-compliant, especially regarding parents.
- Over-concerned for parents.

SOME STRATEGIES THAT CAN BE USED TO ASSIST

If the child is having problems with the family, try to identify the person in the family who is exerting the greatest influence. The strategy to use will depend on the roles of family members.

Try to find other acceptable ways for the child to please the parents. If the child is trying hard but not achieving what the parents want for the child, it may be necessary to approach the parents to help them accept that the child's abilities and interest may not coincide with parental expectations.

Depending on the child's age, use relevant aspects of the values development model to deal effectively with conflict. Help adolescents to 'agree to differ' yet retain respect for parental and cultural values. Help a younger child to accept that different norms may apply in different contexts.

In the case of anxieties involving religious beliefs and related behavioural constraints, it may be very difficult to come to terms with deeply held convictions which differ greatly from those of the professional, whether these stem from one's personal beliefs or from the training and ethos of the profession. In this field it is very difficult to make changes; change comes from within the person's own thinking and is certain to involve a very high level of anxiety in children who question the established customs and beliefs. The professional can help the child to understand that others of different persuasions can also have high moral values, that to differ may also mean to respect. Encourage the child to work through his or her questioning rather than suppress it with feelings of guilt. These are important issues for many adolescents, in many cultures leading to some extreme consequences when traditional religious adherences are rejected.

Problems associated with schooling may be reflected in loss of motivation for achievement in fields other than schooling. Try to ascertain whether the problem is actually as presented by the child. The adolescent may present his or her anxieties as a school problem, whereas further enquiry may reveal that not doing well in school is actually an outcome or a socially acceptable excuse for feelings of anxiety about socially or sexually related problems.

Poor or variable performance not matching the child's abilities may indicate poor learning skills. These can be checked out first with teachers or school counsellors before ascribing failures to anxiety. The child may need special assistance, for example, with English language. Use of a mentor from the same minority group will provide a helpful model for a child from a disadvantaged cultural background.

Do not denigrate high motivation in the anxious child but try to show the child better ways of solving problems, and many other ways of pleasing parents. Encourage a wider range of activities and interests. Help the child organise time spent on home study to be effective and reduce time-wasting distractions. (Schooling issues will be treated more fully in a later volume in the series.)

Social and interpersonal problems are likely to be more apparent in older children and adolescents, but can also occur with younger children. Find out if the child's associates are from the same or another culture. Try to find out who are doing the rejecting and why. The child's interpretation of the relationship may not be as accurate as he or she thinks, but reflects the child's own insecurity as much as others' attitudes.

Adolescents, especially girls, from second-generation immigrant families from traditional cultures often resent the social constraints placed upon them in comparison with their peers from other cultures. Encourage and assist the child to mix with children of other cultures in supportive and non-threatening situations. Try to involve parents, school and community youth groups in activities.

When the child is having difficulty in mixing with other children, it may be that the child is not aware of the social norms of the culture. It could be a relatively simple thing to redress, as, for example, to use more eye contact, or to take a school lunch that will not offend others.

If the child is the butt of more serious prejudice, the work must be done with others as well as with the child. If one of the more influential of the perpetrators can be persuaded to defend the victim, that child will not only become a staunch ally but a powerful agent in reducing the prejudicial attacks. If the social difficulties are from the child's own incorrect perceptions of the situation, work to overcome these problems by assisting the child to change his or her own behaviours. Begin with simple, concrete actions, and help the child to use his or her own cognitive understanding to assess the outcome of each step. Make sure that the child experiences the satisfaction of success before attempting to deal with more complex problems.

There is much professional help available from psychologists and counsellors to deal with more serious social problems.

Problems with cultural identity are most likely to arise when the child comes from a disadvantaged minority or has a mixed cultural heritage. Encourage recognition of and pride in the child's cultural and ethnic background. This is especially important for children of mixed ethnic heritage where one of the child's parents comes from a culture which is not held in high repute by the culture of the other parent. Such children suffer doubly, because their own cultural identity involves both sides. Denial of either is counter-productive but that may be difficult for the child to accept.

Encourage the child to study the culture of its origins. Try to help the child understand that all cultures change over time, and although some of the ways of the past may not be relevant in the present, many aspects of traditional cultures have endured because of the universal human values they embody but which different cultures express in different ways.

Find and encourage appropriate good models from the child's culture. These could be drawn from the literature of the culture, from sport, achievements in the arts and music or contributions to the advancement of the community. The choice will depend on the child's age, gender and personal interests.

This chapter has highlighted culturally related anxieties and worries of ordinary children growing up in mostly normal environments. It has not attempted to deal with the more serious problems or with the effects of traumas of children who have suffered from natural disasters, war and famine, or from life-threatening illnesses, sexual assaults and other aggressive acts. See, for example, Arellano-Carendang's (1987) work with child victims of war and political strife in the Philippines. If the child does not respond to efforts to assist, or if the problem behaviour has continued over a long period, the help of a specialist professional should be sought.

Yet there are many children who have survived severe privations and do not appear to have been permanently damaged. These resilient children are the survivors: they use their determination and resourcefulness to overcome what to most would appear to be insurmountable difficulties. In dealing with the worries and anxieties of ordinary children we may at some time come across such children. They may be among the professionals' regular clientele, but one may not even know it until the child's background is pointed out. We can learn much from these survivors. They can give us heart about the ability of children in so many cultures to overcome their difficulties and grow for the better from having faced and dealt with their problems.

SUGGESTIONS FOR FURTHER READING

Pedersen, P.B., Draguns, J.G., Lonner, W.J. & Trimble, J.E. (Eds), (1989). *Counseling Across Cultures*, 3rd edn. Honolulu: University of Hawaii Press. Chapters on foreign students, Asian-Americans, Hispanic and Native American Indians will be useful.

McInerney, D.M. (1990). The determinants of motivation for urban Aboriginal students: a cross-cultural analysis. *Journal of Cross-Cultural Psychology*, **21**, 474–495.

Kashiwagi, K. (1986). Personality development of adolescents. In H. Stevenson, H. Azuma & K. Hakuta (Eds), *Child Development and Education in Japan*. New York: Freeman, pp. 177–185.

7

MULTICULTURAL INTERACTION AND CULTURAL CHANGE

The previous chapters have brought out many problems involving multicultural interactions between children and adults and other children, and some suggestions to deal with these problems have been put forward to assist professionals working with these children. From that analysis it might seem that the child who is being brought up in a multicultural environment might be certain to experience greater difficulties than the child who knows only one cultural world. Such is not necessarily the case. Experiencing other cultures can be a source of enrichment not matched by the vicarious impressions gained from books, television and films. Moreover, the experience of working with children and their parents from different cultures can be as rewarding for the professional as for the child.

It would be misleading, however, not to face up to the tensions which do exist between the potentially damaging effects of the problems and the potentially enhancing effects of the experience. In this chapter we now take up this question as we review the issues raised in earlier chapters and consider the cultural changes which are likely to affect the child of today as an adult in the twenty-first century.

In the first chapter it was proposed that the professional's role was to help the child cope successfully with the demands of the social world, both within the immediate family and in the wider social context. What would this mean for the child in a multicultural society? Our ideal multicultural child would be more aware of the variety of human experience; would know that people of different cultural background can live in peaceful co-existence; would know that there are many ways of living, and that many religions and differing beliefs about the nature of the world can produce good people even though these religions and beliefs are not the same as the child's. The child will accept that 'different' does not mean 'bad' and 'the same as us' does not mean 'good'.

In a multicultural society intermarriage may occur but is not regarded as intrinsically problematical. If one of this child's parents has married into another ethnic or cultural group, the child would learn the values of its double heritage with pride in both parental backgrounds. This enriched cultural heritage would be taught to the child as a benefit, leading to greater enjoyment of cultural variation and greater tolerance of others.

It would be unrealistic to expect that this idealistic situation will easily occur. Problems will arise for the child if the transmission of awareness of difference is linked to fear of others who are different or leads to the loss of feelings of self-worth. Comparisons which highlight cultural factors in difference could lead instead to prejudice and even violence, as political, ideological, religious and temperamental differences are all interpreted in terms of 'us' and 'them'.

Tensions are present in all new learning and there is no doubt that some new cultural learning can be very difficult for children because so many new things are demanded which tax their cognitive capacity and bewilder them. If the behaviour which is expected of them is very different from what they have been taught by their parents, children will have difficulties in deciding which authority to obey and which models to follow.

New cultural learning can be difficult for older people because of the many threats to old values. The problem of how to maintain what was valued, and ensure that the next generations do not abandon those values, is a source of many conflicts between the older and younger members of the family. In the case of older members of immigrant families and refugees, there may have been inadequate preparation for the new lifestyles now required. Perhaps no one has informed the older parents or grandparents in the home country of the real situation in the country to which they have emigrated with such high hopes. Or they are unable to appreciate the real situation even if others have tried to present a fair picture. The expectation that the new language will be learned with ease may meet with disappointment. Messages from tourist organisations show glowing pictures. Immigration authorities also stress the attractiveness of the country but even if they try to present a more balanced picture may fail to impress on the applicant the problems that will be encountered. For refugees the new country is the 'promised land' and the early euphoria of the arrival may soon give way to disappointment. The feelings have been described as 'culture shock' (Furnham & Bochner, 1986). Another term is 'acculturative stress'. Too often the conditions for guest workers are not what the worker was led to expect, and the problems of the parents can be all too easily transmitted to the children.

For all these reasons the reality of beginning life in a new cultural environment can be very stressful for families. The anxieties of the parents and older family members are readily passed on to the children. They are often expressed in terms of a greater insistence on obedience to the parents' desires for their children's behaviour.

The problems discussed in the preceding chapters are also problems which occur in the longer term after the initial settlement period is over. Although the first stage of acculturation is more dramatic, the slower adjustment also requires much new learning.

THE MAIN THEMES

The focus of this book has been on the role of cultural factors in the child's development. Some themes have recurred in several contexts and relate closely to each other. These are the issues of which the professional who deals with children and their families needs to be particularly aware. It has been a basic thesis of the book that the child must be considered in the context of its family and social environment, not in a static sense but in the dynamic interaction as proposed in Valsiner's (1987) concept of co-construction of the child's world. In that interaction the professional plays an active and integral part.

Most universal in all cultures is the influence of parents on their children. This theme appears in various ways in each chapter. The power of that influence is expressed in the parents' expectations for the child, in the child's concerns about family relationships and in the anxieties which are aroused in some children when attempting to meet those expectations.

As we saw in Chapter 3, the family structure and the goals of development for the children are closely interrelated. The many variants on the family structure mean that caution is needed in considering just what constitutes the family in each case. The roles and status of family members differ greatly across cultures, and the professional must be careful to recognise and respect these differences. One should be particularly cautious about using junior family members as go-betweens to communicate with the senior members. For this reason alone a child should not be used as interpreter when interviewing an adult family member. As was shown when dealing with this issue, other reasons concern the child's inadequate knowledge.

Cultural differences also affect how the parents treat siblings. Both age and gender produce differential treatment and some cultures have very strong markers of sibling roles which the professional needs to understand in dealing with children in the same family.

Cultural differences are found in temperamental and be-havioural styles. However, within all cultures individual dif-ferences must be taken into account. All behavioural variation cannot be attributed to cultural factors.

For adolescents, social interactions can be the sources of many problems, especially when they involve cultural identity, self-esteem, boy–girl relationships and relations with parents. As was shown in Chapter 6, these are adolescent concerns which are found in many different cultures.

Problems relating to the child's sense of cultural identity can arise in many contexts. They can become a source of anxiety for children when the family comes from a disadvantaged background which is frequently the target of prejudice in the majority of the population. Because the knowledge of one's cultural identity is a complex psychological concept, it is not acquired in its complete form in early childhood. It is only when the child has developed conceptually to a stage where cultural differences between self and others are fully under-stood that the nature of the child's own sense of cultural identity is really understood. This is not the same as having knowledge of one's ethnic identity. The distinction between the two concepts was brought out in the treatment of situated identities, which explains how one person might see oneself behaving in different ways in differing cultural contexts. In such situations, behaviour does not change a person's ethnic identity.

Situated identities are not only used by the young but are equally relevant to their parents, who may behave differently towards the child in situations with their own ethnic groups from their behaviour in other contexts. While adaptability to social contexts can be facilitating, lack of consistency in the parents' treatment of the child will be sure to confuse the child. If this changeability occurs in dealing with an adoles-cent's relations with peers, it is likely to encourage resentment and frustration in the young person. The many possible outcomes can be seen in the discussion of children's anxieties in Chapter 6.

One of the persistent themes in previous chapters is the need to encourage respect for the child's cultural heritage. To do this effectively, the child can be supported in learning about its culture in many ways, both formal and informal. It will help both the child and other children to share experiences and knowledge about their culture. The professional also benefits from learning more about the culture of the families. There is no substitute for cultural knowledge.

CULTURAL CHANGE INTO THE TWENTY-FIRST CENTURY

Cultural change is now occurring in all countries so rapidly that many parents cannot imagine what the future will be like for the child of today. Even the most traditional societies are affected. Cultural isolation has gone forever.

The new communications technologies have made it possible for the most remote people to know what is happening in distant parts of the world. Through live television broadcasting, and with computer links such as the Internet and electronic mail, communication can be immediate. Children become accustomed to using these channels very easily, and quickly become far more at home with them than their parents do.

The influence of the mass media has already been felt in all countries. Many countries have resented the power of foreign television shows over indigenous entertainment and their effects upon the young.

International business corporations and advertising target the young people in many countries, with consequent changes in food habits, dress styles and language. These influences are seen by many traditional leaders as dangerous threats to their cultures, and are often countered by greater demands for conforming to traditional practices and values. The youth of the country are frequent targets of these conservative forces.

Public education systems are now universal but in many countries have not been fully implemented. Distance has been a factor in many countries. Poverty prevents many programmes from succeeding, as in many African countries. It seems likely that the present trend of overseas study will continue to increase, adding further to the international influences on indigenous cultures.

One of the greatest effects of the increase in public education comes from the education of girls. Not only will the women of the twenty-first century have better access to knowledge about child rearing, but they will also have a wider general knowledge and demand more opportunities for advanced study and professional occupations. These opportunities already exist in some cultures but in others there is still much ignorance and discrimination in favour of males.

It has been shown in research (e.g. LeVine, 1989) that one of the most outstanding outcomes of introducing education programmes for women and girls has been the greater knowledge of the need for population control. In multicultural societies, where some women have more freedom than others in regard to birth control and related sexual practices, there is likely to be conflict between the educated women and the authorities who inhibit change through religious or other cultural taboos. It is not clear to what degree these conflicts will be resolved for the girls of today in their adulthood.

We can also expect that the next century will demand new types of skill which will displace many traditional methods in the workplace. To some extent the international commercial organisations will lead these demands. The effect in many cultures will be an erosion of traditional skills and an increase in migration from villages to the cities. The children of today will become the urban migrants and sojourners of tomorrow.

Along with the spread of education and access to information, we can expect improvements in public health systems. Already there is evidence of a general increase in the life span. The better diet of today's children and the control of infectious diseases have also improved the quality of public health in many countries, although, as we are only too aware, these benefits are not experienced by children in all countries.

International travel has now opened up to many people the opportunity to experience other cultures. As these opportunities increase, knowledge of other cultures will become more necessary, and more accessible. Knowledge of another language will be an even greater asset than it is now.

There is no doubt that the increase in the knowledge base, the opening up of different cultural experiences and the need for new skills will challenge many traditional cultural beliefs and practices. It could be that in some cases a scientific basis will be found for some traditional practices which previously depended for their acceptance on knowledge handed down by traditional gurus, healers and religious leaders. On the other hand, scepticism can lead to the search for truth, with the result that some other beliefs and practices will be discarded as inappropriate for the modern world.

As has been shown in previous chapters, evidence from many countries – for example, Greece, India, Japan, Thailand which have been highly traditional in the strength of family relationships – shows that the extended family structure is losing its influence. Families are still close in their interpersonal contacts but traditional hierarchical power structures are being eroded.

The picture presented here of the adult world of today's children suggests that the cultural gap between children and their parents will become even wider than it is now. However, more intercultural interaction does not necessarily lead to more cultural understanding. Professionals who work with children of many different cultural backgrounds have a unique opportunity to help those children appreciate the cultural heritages of their own families and the families of others. As was stressed in earlier chapters, to respect the culture of others does not mean that one always has to agree with all their beliefs and practices. That all cultures change over time is inevitable, and because cultural change is now occurring so rapidly it is well to prepare children for a world that will be very different from the world their parents knew.

THE PROFESSIONAL'S ROLE

The aim of this book is to be a practical guide rather than a definitive academic text. It is intended to help professionals cope with cultural change as well as personal problems. Research backs all that has been offered, but the number of references in the text has been kept as low as possible in the interest of ease of use. Those readers who want to dig deeper are urged to follow up the suggestions for further reading supplied at the end of chapters. If, by this approach, the writer has been briefer than would be necessary to do justice to a particular issue, it has been in order to make the book a resource that will not stay on a library shelf but will become a guide to practical help in everyday use.

Because this is neither a textbook in child development nor a research monograph, the topics included have been carefully selected, placing an emphasis on the kind of issues that occur in professional practice. The reader will not have found a chapter on cognitive development as there have been many cross-cultural studies on this theme, and although many interesting differences are found, it is clear that these differences have their basis in those things the culture values as worth learning and thinking about. There are as many individual differences among children in all cultures as there are performance differences among cultures. Wherever they happen to be, the children will respond to the demands the culture places upon them. This theme will no doubt be treated more thoroughly in the volume on culture and schooling.

The book is addressed to professionals in child care and child development. Who are these professionals? There are so many people who work with children that some may not see themselves in the category which is so loosely termed 'professional'. Each type of work has its own agenda, its own style of working and its own training. However, in their common concern for the welfare of children there will be a wealth of shared experience. The child's problem does not change because of the professional who is assigned to deal with it. What changes is the representation of the problem and the repertoire of responses which different professional orientations bring to dealing with the problem. The effect can be that each professional sees the problem from his or her own point of view rather than from that of the child. The more hands the problem goes through, the more does the difficulty of the child increase. However, in some cases the redefinition of a problem can bring new insights, leading to a solution as new ways of perceiving the issues are revealed. It is hoped that this more productive approach may come from sharing some of the ideas presented in this book.

In writing for professionals who work in many different cultural environments and under a range of employment conditions, it has been inevitable that not all the issues will have the same relevance to all situations. The reader is asked to take up what is immediately useful, but it is hoped that the major thrust of the book will have some generalisability in bringing to professionals, in their daily work or training, an appreciation for the role that culture plays in the life of the child. At the least may it promote a lively discussion of this important aspect of the life of every child.

REFERENCES

Aboud, F.E. & Skerry, S.A. (1984). The development of ethnic attitudes: a critical review. *Journal of Cross-Cultural Psychology*, **15**, 3–34.

Arellano-Carendang, M.L. (1987). *Filipino Children under Stress*. Quezon City: Ateneo de Manila University Press.

Ateca, B., Sunar, D. & Kağitçibaşi, Ç. (1994). Variance in fertility due to sex-related differentiation in child-rearing practices. Poster presentation, Twelfth Congress of the International Association for Cross-Cultural Psychology, Pamplona, Spain.

Axia, G., Prior, M. & Carelli, M.G. (1992). Cultural influences on temperament: a comparison of Italian, Italo-Australian, and Anglo-Australian toddlers. *Australian Psychologist*, **27**, 52–56.

Bandura, A. (1986). *The Social Foundations of Thought and Action: A Social Cognitive Theory*. Englewood Cliffs, NJ: Prentice Hall.

Berry, J.W., Poortinga, Y.P., Segall, M.H. & Dasen, P.R. (1992). *Cross-Cultural Psychology: Research and Applications*. Cambridge: Cambridge University Press.

Bertelli, L. (1985). Italian families. In D. Storer (Ed.), *Ethnic Family Values in Australia*. Sydney: Prentice Hall.

Blue, A.W., Corenblum, B. & Annis, R.C. (1987). Developmental trends in racial preference and identification in northern native Canadian children. In Ç. Kağitçibaşi (Ed.), *Growth and Progress in Cross-Cultural Psychology*. Lisse: Swets & Zeitlinger, pp. 311–320.

Bornstein, M.H. (1995). Form and function: implications for studies of culture and human development. *Culture and Psychology*, **1**, 123–137.

Bornstein, M.H., Azuma, H., Tamis-LeMonda, C. & Ogino, M. (1990a). Mother and infant activity and interaction in Japan and the United States: I. A comparative macroanalysis of naturalistic exchanges. *International Journal of Behavioural Development*, **13**, 267–287.

Bornstein, M.H., Toda, S., Azuma, H., Tamis-LeMonda, C. & Ogino, M. (1990b). Mother and infant activity and interaction in Japan and the United States: II. A comparative microanalysis of naturalistic exchanges focused on the organisation of infant attention. *International Journal of Behavioural Development, 13*, 289–308.

Brislin, R. (1990). *Applied Cross-Cultural Psychology.* Newbury Park, CA: Sage.

Burns, A. (1991). When is a family? In K. Funder (Ed.), *Images of Australian Families.* pp. 23–38. Melbourne: Longmans Cheshire.

Burns, A. & Goodnow, J.J. (1979). *Children and Families in Australia.* Sydney: Allen & Unwin.

Carey, W.B. & McDevitt, S.C. (1978). Revision of the infant temperament scale. *Pediatrics, 68*, 735–739.

Cashmore, J.A. & Goodnow, J.J. (1986). Parent–child agreement on attributional beliefs. *International Journal of Behavioural Development, 9*, 191–204.

Child Development Centre of China (1993). *A Compilation of the Theses of CDCC in the Past Decade, 1983–1993,* English edition. Beijing: Child Development Centre of China.

Chiam, H.K. (1984). Profile of rural adolescents in Malaysia. In Y.C. Leong, H.K. Chiam & L.S.M. Chew (Eds), *Preparation for Adulthood.* Kuala Lumpur: University of Malaya, pp. 323–337.

Clark, K. & Clark, M. (1939). The development of consciousness of self and the emergence of racial identification in Negro pre-school children. *Journal of Social Psychology, 10*, 591–599.

Clark, K.B. & Clark, M.P. (1947). Racial identification and preference in Negro children. In T.M. Newcomb & E.L. Hartley (Eds), *Readings in Social Psychology.* New York: Holt, Rhinehart, pp. 169–178.

Crystal, D.S., Chen, C.-S., Fuligni, A., Stevenson, H.W., Hsu, C.-C., Ko, H.-J., Kitamura, S. & Kitamura, S. (1994). Psychological maladjustment and academic achievement: a cross-cultural study of Japanese, Chinese, and American high school students. *Child Development, 65*, 738–753.

Doi, T. (1981). *The Anatomy of Dependence,* revised edn. Tokyo: Kodansha International.

Ekstrand, L.H. (Ed.) (1986). *Ethnic Minorities and Immigrants in a Cross-Cultural Perspective.* Lisse: Swets & Zeitlinger.

Eldering, L. (1991). Intervention programmes for pre-schoolers from immigrant families: the Dutch case. In N. Bleichrodt & P.J.D. Drenth (Eds), *Contemporary Issues in Cross-Cultural Psychology.* Amsterdam: Swets & Zeitlinger, pp. 64–71.

Fang, F.-X. & Keats, D.M. (1989). The Master and the Wolf: a study in the development of social perspective taking in Chinese and Australian children. In D.M. Keats, D. Munro & L. Mann (Eds), *Heterogeneity in Cross-Cultural Psychology,* Amsterdam: Swets & Zeitlinger, pp. 419–425.

Feather, N.T. (1989). Attitudes towards the high achiever: the fall of the tall poppy. *Australian Journal of Psychology*, **41**, 239–268.

Funder, K. (Ed.) (1991). *Images of Australian Families*. Melbourne: Longmans Cheshire.

Furnham, A. & Bochner, S. (1986). *Culture Shock: Psychological Reactions to Unfamiliar Environments*. London: Methuen.

Geertz, H. (1982). *The Javanese Family*, revised edn. New York: Glencoe Free Press.

Georgas, J. (1989). Changing family values in Greece. *Journal of Cross-Cultural Psychology*, **20**, 80–91.

Georgas, J. & Papastylianou, D. (1994). The effect of time on stereotypes: acculturation of children of returning immigrants to Greece. In A.-M. Bouvy, F.J.R. van de Vijver, P. Boski & P. Schmitz (Eds), *Journeys into Cross-Cultural Psychology*. Lisse: Swets & Zeitlinger, pp. 158–166.

George, D.M. & Hoppe, R.A. (1979). Racial identification, preference, and self-concept. *Journal of Cross-Cultural Psychology*, **10**, 85–100.

Gibson, J.I., Westwood, M.J., Ishiyama, F.I., Borgen, W.A. *et al.* (1991). Youth and culture: a seventeen nation study of perceived problems and coping strategies. *International Journal for the Advancement of Counselling*, **14**, 203–216.

Hatzichristou, C. & Hopf, D. (1995). School adaptation of Greek children after remigration: age differences in multiple domains. *Journal of Cross-Cultural Psychology*, **26**, 505–522.

Ho, D.Y.F. (1974). Face, social expectations, and conflict avoidance. In J.L.M. Dawson & W.J. Lonner (Eds), *Readings in Cross-Cultural Psychology*. Hong Kong: Hong Kong University Press, pp. 240–251.

Ho, D.Y.F. (1986). Chinese patterns of socialization: a critical review. In M.H. Bond (Ed.), *The Psychology of the Chinese People*. Hong Kong: Oxford University Press, pp. 1–37.

Ho, D.Y.F. (1994). Filial piety, authoritarian moralism and cognitive conservatism in Chinese societies. *Genetic, Social and General Psychology Monographs*, 349–365.

Kağitçibaşi, Ç. (1994). Human development and societal development. In A.-M. Bouvy, F.J.R. van de Vijver, P. Boski & P. Schmitz (Eds), *Journeys in Cross-Cultural Psychology*, Lisse: Swets & Zeitlinger, pp. 3–24.

Kağitçibaşi, Ç. (1995). *Family and Human Development across Cultures: A view from the Other Side*. New Jersey: Erlbaum.

Kakar, S. (1979). Childhood in India: traditional ideals and contemporary reality. *International Social Science Journal*, **31**, 444–456.

Kashiwagi, K. (1986). Personality development in adolescents. In H. Stevenson, H. Azuma & K. Hakuta (Eds), *Child Development and Education in Japan*, New York: Freeman, pp. 167–185.

Keats, D.M. (1981). The development of values. In J.L.M. Binnie-Dawson, G.H. Blowers & R. Hoosain (Eds), *Perspectives in Asian Cross-Cultural Psychology*. Lisse: Swets & Zeitlinger, pp. 68–95.

Keats, D.M. (1986). Using the cross-cultural method to study the development of values. *Australian Journal of Psychology*, **38**, 297–308.

Keats, D.M. & Fang, F.-X. (1992). The effect of modification of stimulus materials on the social perspective taking ability of Chinese and Australian children. In S. Iwawaki, Y. Kashima & K. Leung (Eds), *Innovations in Cross-Cultural Psychology*. Amsterdam: Swets & Zeitlinger, pp. 319–327.

Keats, D.M. & Fang, F.-X. (1996). The development of concepts of fairness in rewards in Chinese and Australian children. In H. Grad, A. Blanco & J. Georgas (Eds), *Key Issues in Cross-Cultural Psychology*. Amsterdam: Swets & Zeitlinger, pp. 276–287.

Keller, H. & Eibl-Eibesfeldt, I. (1989). Concepts of parenting: the role of eye contact in early parent–child interaction. In D.M. Keats, D. Munro & L. Mann (Eds), *Heterogeneity in Cross-Cultural Psychology*. Amsterdam: Swets & Zeitlinger, pp. 468–476.

Keller, H., Schölmerich, A. & Eibl-Eibesfeldt, I. (1988). Communication patterns in adult–infant interaction in Western and non-Western cultures. *Journal of Cross-Cultural Psychology*, **19**, 427–445.

Kelly, G.A. (1955). *The Psychology of Personal Constructs*. New York: Norton.

Kelman, H.C. (1961). Processes of opinion change. *Public Opinion Quarterly*, **25**, 57–78.

Koops, W., Soppe, H.J.G., van der Linden, J.L., Molenaar, P.C.M. & Schroots, J.J.F. (Eds) (1990). *Developmental Psychology behind the Dikes: An Outline of Developmental Psychological Research in the Netherlands*. Delft: Uitgeverij Eburon.

Kornadt, H.-J. (1991). Aggression motive and its developmental conditions in eastern and western cultures. In N. Bleichrodt & P.J.D. Drenth (Eds), *Contemporary Issues in Cross-Cultural Psychology*. Amsterdam: Swets & Zeitlinger, pp. 155–167.

Kornadt, H.-J., Hayashi, T., Tachibana, Y., Trommsdorff, G. & Yamauchi, H. (1992). Aggressiveness and its developmental conditions in five cultures. In S. Iwawaki, Y. Kashima & K. Leung (Eds), *Innovations in Cross-Cultural Psychology*. Amsterdam: Swets & Zeitlinger, pp. 250–268.

Krolik, P. (1981). Sex role perceptions of educated young women from five cultures. Unpublished M.Sc. Thesis, University of Newcastle, Australia.

Lazarevic, R. (1992). The self-esteem of rural and urban Aboriginal school students in New South Wales. Unpublished M. Psych. (Ed.) Thesis, University of Newcastle, Australia.

LeVine, R.A. (1989). Maternal schooling and reproduction in developing countries. In D.M. Keats, D. Munro & L. Mann (Eds), *Heterogeneity in Cross-Cultural Psychology*. Amsterdam: Swets & Zeitlinger, pp. 462–467.

Liddell, C., Kvalsvig, J., Shababala, A. & Masilela, P. (1991). Historical perspectives on South African childhood. *International Journal of Behavioural Development*, **14**, 1–19.

Markus, H.R. & Kitayama, S. (1991). Culture and the self: implications for cognition, emotion and motivation. *Psychological Review*, **98**, 224–253.

McDonald, P. (1991). Migrant family structure. In K. Funder (Ed.), *Images of Australian Families*. Melbourne: Longmans Cheshire, pp. 102–121.

McInerney, D.M. (1990). The determinants of motivation for urban Aboriginal students: a cross-cultural analysis. *Journal of Cross-Cultural Psychology*, **21**, 474–495.

Meng, Z.-L. (1994). The only children's early rearing in urban China. Unpublished paper presented to the 13th Biennial Meeting of the International Society for the Study of Behavioural Development, Amsterdam.

Mulder, N. (1992a). *Individual and Society in Java*, revised edn. Jogjakarta: Gajah Mada University Press.

Mulder, N. (1992b). *Inside South-East Asia: Thai, Javanese and Filipino Interpretations of Everyday Life*. Bangkok: Editions Duang Kamol.

Munroe, R.L. & Munroe, R.H. (1994). *Cross-cultural Human Development*, revised edn. Prospect Heights, IL: Waveland Press.

Naidoo, J.C. (1985). A cultural perspective on the adjustment of South Asian women in Canada. In I. Reyes Lagunes & Y.H. Poortinga (Eds), *From a Different Perspective: Studies of Behavior Across Cultures*. Lisse: Swets & Zeitlinger, pp. 76–92.

Naidoo, J.C. (1986). Value conflicts for South Asian women in multicultural Canada. In L.H. Ekstrand (Ed.), *Ethnic Minorities and Immigrants in a Cross-Cultural Perspective*. Lisse: Swets & Zeitlinger, pp. 132–146.

Naidoo, J.C. & Davis, J.C. (1988). Canadian South Asian women in transition: a dualistic view of life. *Journal of Comparative Family Studies*, **19**, 311–327.

Nsamenang, A.B. (1992). *Human Development in Cultural Context: A Third World Perspective*. Thousand Oaks, CA: Sage.

Nsamenang, A.B. (1995). Theories of developmental psychology from a cultural perspective: a viewpoint from Africa. *Psychology and Developing Societies*, **7**, 1–19.

Nsamenang, A.B. & Lamb, M.E. (1993). The acquisition of socio-cognitive competence by NSO children in the Bamenda Grasslands of Northwest Cameroon. *International Journal of Behavioural Development*, **16**, 429–441.

Öner, N. & Tosün, U. (1991). Adjustment of the children of re-migrant workers in Turkey: A comparison of immigrant and non-migrant Turkish adolescents. In N. Bleichrodt & P.J.D. Drenth (Eds), *Contemporary Issues in Cross-Cultural Psychology*. Amsterdam: Swets & Zeitlinger, pp. 155–167.

Pedersen, P.B., Draguns, J.G., Lonner, W.J. & Trimble, J.E. (Eds) (1989). *Counseling Across Cultures*, 3rd edn. Honolulu: University of Hawaii Press.

Pels, T. (1991). Developmental expectations of Moroccan and Dutch parents. In N. Bleichrodt & P.J.D. Drenth (Eds), *Contemporary Issues in Cross-Cultural Psychology*. Lisse: Swets & Zeitlinger, pp. 64–71.

Phinney, J.S., DuPont, S., Espinosa, C., Revill, J. & Sanders, K. (1994). Ethnic identity and American identification among ethnic minority youths. In A.-M. Bouvy, F.J.R. van de Vijver, P. Boski & P. Schmitz (Eds), *Journeys in Cross-Cultural Psychology*, Amsterdam: Swets & Zeitlinger, pp. 167–183.

Piaget, J. (1932). *The Moral Judgement of the Child*. London: Routledge & Kegan Paul.

Piaget, J. (1981). *Intelligence and Affectivity: Their Relationship during Child Development* (translated and edited by T.A. Brown & C.E. Kaegi). Palo Alto, CA: Annual Reviews Inc.

Piaget, J. & Weil, A.J. (1951). The development of children's ideas of the homeland and of relations to other countries. *International Social Science Journal*, **3**, 561–578.

Power, T.G., Kobayashi-Winata, H. & Kelley, M.L. (1992). Childrearing patterns in Japan and the United States: a cluster analytic study. *International Journal of Behavioural Development*, **15**, 185–205.

Prior, M., Guarino, E., Sanson, A. & Oberklaid, F. (1987a). Ethnic influences on 'difficult' temperament and behavioural problems. *Australian Journal of Psychology*, **39**, 163–171.

Prior, M.R., Kyrios, M. & Oberklaid, F. (1986). Temperament in Australian, American, Chinese and Greek infants: some issues and directions for future research. *Journal of Cross-Cultural Psychology*, **17**, 455–474.

Prior, M., Sanson, A. & Oberklaid, F. (1989). The Australian temperament project. In G. Kohnstamm, J. Bates & M. Rothbart (Eds), *Temperament in Childhood*. Chichester: Wiley, pp. 537–554.

Prior, M., Sanson, A., Oberklaid, F. & Northam, E. (1987b). Measurement of temperament in 1 to 3 year old children. *International Journal of Behavioural Development*, **10**, 121–132.

Rosenthal, D.A., Demetriou, A. & Efklides, A. (1989). A crossnational study of the influence of culture on conflict between parents and adolescents. *International Journal of Behavioural Development*, **12**, 207–219.

Rutherford, G.D. (1993). The development of concepts of cultural identity in Thai and Australian school students. Unpublished Ph.D. Thesis, University of Newcastle, Australia.

Saraswathi, T.S. & Dutta, R. (1987). Cross-cultural research in developmental psychology: retrospect and prospect in India. In Ç. Kağitçibaşi (Ed.), *Growth and Progress in Cross-Cultural Psychology*. Lisse: Swets & Zeitlinger, pp. 148–158.

Schmitz, P. (1992). Acculturation styles and health. In S. Iwawaki, Y. Kashima & K. Leung (Eds), *Innovations in Cross-Cultural Psychology*. Amsterdam: Swets & Zeitlinger, pp. 152–163.

Segall, M.H., Dasen, P., Berry, J.W. & Poortinga, Y.H. (Eds) (1990). *Human Behavior in Global Perspective: An Introduction to Cross-Cultural Psychology*. New York: Pergamon.

Selman, R.L. (1980). *The Growth of Interpersonal Understanding*. New York: Academic Press.

Setiono, K. (1994). An indigenous approach to Javanese adolescents. Unpublished paper in the Symposium on Indigenous Approaches to Developmental Psychology, 13th Biennial Meeting of the International Society for the Study of Behavioural Development, Amsterdam, July.

Sinha, S.R. (1995). Childrearing practices relevant to the growth of dependency and competence in children. In J. Valsiner (Ed.), *Child Development within Culturally Structured Environments*. Vol. 3, *Comparative-Cultural and Constructivist Perspectives*. New Jersey: Ablex, pp. 105–137.

Skolnick, A.S. (1986). *The Psychology of Human Development*. New York: Harcourt Brace Jovanovich.

Stevenson, H., Azuma, A. & Hakuta, K. (Eds) (1986). *Child Development and Education in Japan*. New York: Freeman.

Storer, D. (Ed.) (1985). *Ethnic Family Values in Australia*. Sydney: Prentice Hall.

Suvannathat, C., Bhanthumnavin, D., Bhuapirom, L. & Keats, D.M. (Eds) (1985). *Handbook of Asian Child Development and Child Rearing Practices*. Bangkok: Behavioral Science Research Institute.

Thomas, D.R. (1986). Culture and ethnicity: maintaining the distinction. *Australian Journal of Psychology*, **38**, 371–380.

Thomas, A., Chess, S. & Birch, H.G. (1970). The origin of personality. *Scientific American*, **223**(2). Cited in A.S. Skolnick (1986), *The Psychology of Human Development*. New York: Harcourt Brace Jovanovich.

Valsiner, J. (1987). *Culture and the Development of Children's Action: A Cultural–Historical Theory of Developmental Psychology*. Chichester: Wiley.

Valsiner, J. (Ed.) (1995). *Child Development within Culturally Structured Environments. Vol. 3: Comparative-Cultural and Constructivist Perspectives*. New Jersey: Ablex.

Vanindananda, N.M.S. (1985). Social perspective taking. In C. Suvannathat, D. Bhanthumnavin, L. Bhuapirom & D.M. Keats (Eds), *Handbook of Asian Child Development and Child Rearing Practices*. Bangkok: Behavioral Science Research Institute.

Verma, J. (1995). The transformation of women's roles in India. In J. Valsiner (Ed.), *Child Development within Culturally Structured Environments. Vol. 3: Comparative-Cultural and Constructivist Perspectives*. New Jersey: Ablex, pp. 138–163.

Weinreich, P. (1986). Identity development in migrant offspring: Theory and practice. In L.H. Ekstrand (Ed.), *Ethnic Minorities and Immigrants in a Cultural Perspective*. Lisse: Swets & Zeitlinger, pp. 230–239.

Weinreich, P., Kelly, A. & Maja, C. (1987). Situated identities, conflicts in identification and own group preference: rural and urban youth in South Africa. In Ç. Kağitçibaşi (Ed.), *Growth and Progress in Cross-Cultural Psychology*. Lisse: Swets & Zeitlinger, pp. 321–326.

White, M.J. & LeVine, R.A. (1986). What is an *ii ko* (good child)? In H. Stevenson, H. Azuma & K. Hakuta (Eds), *Child Development and Education in Japan*. New York: Freeman, pp. 55–62.

Williams, J.E. & Best, D.L. (1982). *Measuring Sex Stereotypes: A Thirty Nation Study*. Beverly Hills, CA.: Pergamon.

Wingerson, L. (1990). *Mapping Our Genes: The Genome Project and the Future of Medicine*. New York: Dutton.

Zhang, Y., Kohnstamm, G.A. & van der Kamp, L.T.T. (1993). Temperament difference in young Chinese children. In *A Compilation of the Theses of CDCC in the Past Decade, 1983–1993*, English edn. Beijing: Child Development Centre of China, pp. 135–151.

AUTHOR INDEX

SUBJECT INDEX